Other Titles by Paul Hersey

Non Fiction
Where the Mountains Throw Their Dice
High Misadventure
Searching for Groundswell
Our Mountains
Merino Country

Anthologies
To the Mountains (edited with Laurence Fearnley)

Guidebooks
Northern Rock (with Ton Snelder)
New Zealand's Great Walks (with Shelley Hersey)

Fiction
Protection

The Cold Inside

a story about mountains, friendship, and doubt

Paul Hersey

The Cold Inside: A Story About Mountains, Friendship, and Doubt is published under Karanema, a sectionalized division under Di Angelo Publications, Inc.

Karanema is an imprint of Di Angelo Publications.
Copyright 2022.
All rights reserved.
Printed in the United States of America.

Di Angelo Publications
4265 San Felipe #1100
Houston, Texas 77027

Library of Congress
The Cold Inside: A Story About Mountains,
Friendship, and Doubt
ISBN: 978-1-955690-18-8
Paperback

Words: Paul Hersey
Cover Design: Savina Deianova
Interior Design: Kimberly James
Editors: Ashley Crantas, Willy Rowberry

Downloadable via Kindle, NOOK, iBooks, and Google Play.

For educational, business, and bulk orders, contact sales@diangelopublications.com.

1. Biography & Autobiography --- Adventurers & Explorers
2. Sports & Recreation --- Mountaineering
3. Sports & Recreation --- Rock Climbing

ABOUT THE AUTHOR

Paul Hersey has worked as a newspaper reporter, ice climbing instructor, surf lifeguard, commercial fisher, enforcement officer, and photographer. He has climbed extensively in New Zealand and overseas for the past thirty years, completing numerous first ascents. Hersey is an award-winning journalist and author; he has contributed to magazines such as *Alpinist*, *New Zealand Geographic*, *The Surfer's Journal*, *North and South*, and *Wilderness*. He lives on the South Island of New Zealand with his partner, next to the sea and close to the mountains.

PART ONE

For they are the broken castles
that bind our land and our hearts firm

ONE

What is the right or wrong of it?

Who gets to judge?

It's certainly not any figure of God, for he or she does not live up there in the clouds above the mountains, surrounding themselves with all variation of fire and brimstone.

And there's no fleet-footed Devil neither, none other than the translucence we face when looking into this veneer of ice.

There is only the greyness within ourselves and a choosing that is not so certain.

I don't often remember dreams, but when I do, they can leave a lasting impression.

My favourite dreams are usually of flying, drifting like a bird high above the land with the ability to view everything and the opportunity to go anywhere.

My worst dreams tend to involve me being chased by

someone or something that I can't see. In others, a loved one is in danger, but I am unable to save them. And then there are the dreams where I am falling, dreams that a climber would rather not have and prefer not to remember.

In *this* dream, I was floating. There was a sensation of bobbing up and down and the sound of trickling water. It didn't seem like a surfing dream—they're also high on my favourites list—but everything was so vivid. Even one of my hands felt wet.

Then I heard a voice: '*Pauuuul...*'

I recognised it as belonging to my friend Jamie, but I couldn't see him. Anyway, what was he doing in my floating dream? Maybe we *were* surfing after all.

'Paul!'

The insistence of the voice roused me awake. It took a few more drowsy moments to work out that, yep, my hand really was wet, there really was trickling water, and I really was floating.

Jamie was also really close. Actually, he was leaning over me and shaking my shoulder.

'Paul! Wake up, will you! There's a river running through the tent!'

Only an optimistic person would have believed that the weather forecast for the weekend was good enough to go mountain climbing. Jamie Vinton-Boot *was* that person. He had a knack for visualising opportunities, however brief, and despite any conviction on my part that the perceived window was about to slam shut. This pretty much summed up our personalities. I reckon it's also part of the reason why we made for a balanced climbing team.

Jamie had shown me the weather map a few days earlier.

No doubt realising that I would judge it as a *non*-window, he'd begun his 'eternal optimist' routine.

'I just want to keep going up to the point that I can't,' he'd proclaimed before I'd had a chance to state the obvious. 'That way I'll know we've pushed it as far as we can. I'll be satisfied with that.'

I'd replied with my usual 'likelihood and consequence' counterargument, and Jamie had only shaken his head. So, I'd then moved on to 'the positive power of negative thinking', something I'd heard in a talk by the Canadian alpinist, Will Gadd, about safe decision-making in the mountains. Essentially, I took Gadd's reasoning to mean that pessimism was an acceptable strategy for self-preservation.

But, as was also usual, Jamie's youthful enthusiasm outlasted my 'old-man' negativity. I'd made a deal out of sighing, and then nodding, at the same time telling myself that, if nothing else, at least it'd be a decent fitness trip. Trying to keep up with Jamie in the hills was always a fitness trip.

'You do get on a bit of a downer about the weather, don't you?' my friend said as we started wandering up the Hopkins Valley in what appeared to me to be suspiciously waning sunshine.

'I hate getting spanked by shitty conditions is all,' I replied. 'If I can climb something on a bluebird day, I'd rather wait. One less thing to worry about seems like common sense, mate.'

Jamie looked at me, but he didn't feel the need to say anything else. Clearly, he figured a better reply was to increase his already brisk walking pace. I put my head down and concentrated on not being left behind.

Dark clouds—'as per the forecast,' I felt the need to mention—loomed over the mountain summits by the time we reached Thomson Stream. The wind also increased its kerfuffle from the northwest. Our goal, Mount Williams, was nowhere to be seen.

'Stop worrying,' Jamie assured me, a hint of a smile revealing that he now also accepted the weather could go either way. 'I'm sure it'll clear up again, bro,' he added.

The first drops of rain started to fall soon after. For whatever reason—call it stubbornness on my part, or perhaps the fact that Jamie had the car keys in his backpack—we kept slogging up the steep, forested hill into increasing murk.

'Well, we've come this far,' Jamie proclaimed, pausing mid-grab between branches to look back down and give me a wink. 'Be rude not to take a peek at the tops, don't you reckon?'

'Like we're going to see anything up there,' I replied with a condescending smile back. Then I laughed. Getting into the hills was generally good for the soul, whatever the weather or conditions.

I didn't stop following Jamie up the hill that gloomy afternoon; I just made a note to find a particularly sheltered location to pitch the tent.

And so, at around 2:00 a.m., after half a night of persistent, if not torrential, rainfall, and with runoff pouring into the previously 'dry' creek bed I had so carefully selected, and despite my boots and other essentials attempting to float off into the darkness, all I could do in my half-awake, dream-confused state was start giggling like an idiot.

'Jesus, Hersey!' Jamie groaned, at the same time trying to locate his head torch in what was threatening to become a mini tsunami. 'Get a grip, mate. Bloody grab something, will you!'

While some climbers are driven by the pursuit of technical difficulty, or to claim each summit they reach as a type of conquest, I am drawn more towards the characteristics of an environment. I search for features on a mountain that will inspire me: perhaps a sharp-edged spur highlighted by early morning sunlight; an angled facet on an otherwise unblemished shield of rock; or a streak of ice that appears more like a lightning strike than something to be climbed. I am searching for aesthetics to base my adventures on. Rather than having the drive to dominate a mountain, or to tick harder and harder grades, for me, there needs to be a personal connection to a particular place.

Mount Williams is a laid-back slab of lichen-splotched greywacke. Its southern rump is skirted at half-height by the Foster Glacier, a poor remnant of the monstrous ice fields that once covered much more of New Zealand. The glacier is pitted with rock fall and sunken to its core from the heat of the sun—the ravages of time increasingly apparent in it, just as they are in all of us.

One of the more prominent mountains in the Hopkins Valley, Mount Williams is also perhaps one of the more reposed. And especially so when viewed from the south. There's nothing particularly ominous about the mountain's stature, unlike its neighbour, Mount Ward, which has a dour—and suitably feisty for those who attempt to climb it in winter—southeast face. A previous trip resulting in frostbitten toes and a painful year of recovery can attest to that!

Along with an almost-welcoming appearance, what also attracted me to Williams was its aspect. Aspect and weathering on greywacke, the most common type of rock found on New

Zealand's mountains, are of particular importance to any climber who might wish to climb it. To find the best alpine rock, we need to become an odd breed of rock hound. We need to understand how greywacke forms, that it is layered like sheets of pastry, then compressed over time like all sandstone, and likely flakey on the edges.

Because of the variable nature of our alpine rock, most mountaineers in New Zealand stick to the ice and snow or to rock routes they know have been climbed before. Or they wait until winter, when the fractured stone is frozen together. But not all greywacke is unreliable. While one side of a mountain like Williams is likely the sharp end of the layering—the consistency of breakfast cereal—a solid, compact weathering rind can form on the opposite side. Signs of pinkish, orange, or red rock means there might be good climbing.

In addition to my aesthetic rock hounding tendencies, I find myself bestowing mountains with human attributes. In my mind, this personification makes them easier to understand. Their form takes on character: a *frowning* wall; a *reluctant* gully; *broad* shoulders. My perception of the mountain's mood provides something else to measure my decision-making and motivation against.

Typically, the first view of any mountain is from a distant perspective. It may seem two-dimensional from such a long way away, but already I am trying to ascertain what mood the mountain is in. What type of face has been revealed? What feature on it do I find appealing?

Drawing closer, I keep checking if the mood remains the same, or if it changes as the aspect of the mountain changes. Some parts of it become more obvious, others less so. Perhaps the change is only subtle, or perhaps it comes with a sudden realisation. Sunlight might brighten the face, highlighting certain features, or a dark cloud draws ominously near. I am trying to consider the potential of the route, where its flaws or challenges exist, before becoming absorbed in the miniature of climbing it.

But, of course, these moods I attempt to ascertain never last. Conditions on the mountain are always changing. I hope that, although we meet as strangers, we might share quality time together, and then part as friends.

In the black rain beneath Mount Williams, Jamie and I managed to locate all of our gear, throw it on top of our now wet sleeping bags and mats, and then drag the tent to higher ground. The only site we could find in the darkness was the top of a rocky knoll, lumpy as all hell. I don't think I managed any more dreaming that night.

Not surprisingly, dawn arrived in a similar bleary-eyed, insipid mood. The torso of Williams rose above us, out of focus either because of the cloud or my lack of sleep, with fresh snow across its shoulders and more cloud curving over its summit like a snug-fitting beanie. Clouds also shielded the horizon to the north, reinforcing the barrier between land and sky, and their presence served as another reminder that there was never enough time.

A shower passed overhead, its raindrops heavy as they slapped against the skin of our tent and onto a sodden ground. Then a squall of wind approached. It careered down the valley with all the commotion of a passing train, shaking our cocoon like we were caught in its draft.

'No rush, then,' Jamie mumbled from deep inside his

sleeping bag. I was surprised at my friend's apparent lack of motivation. Maybe, like me, he was feeling tired after such an eventful night. Perhaps there *were* limits to his enthusiasm.

'Nah, mate,' I replied. 'I guess you'll be wanting another coffee.'

The wind eased later in the morning, and enough warmth spread through the tent to encourage me to poke my head out. There was a sliver of light across Williams and the neighbouring mountains, revealing what the remainder of the day might bring. Could it be worth venturing higher? Even, as Jamie would say, if it was just for a look.

If a climber wants to understand mountains, they must also understand weather. On a settled day, with a bluest-of-blue sky and the high country a contrast of dark rock ridges and bright snow flanks, the decision to climb seems obvious. Conversely, when rain pelts down with the intensity of a waterfall and the wind threatens to throw you from your feet at every step, clearly it's time to head home. But an in-between day like the one Jamie and I were experiencing feels like being caught in a perpetual grey zone. *What do we do?*

It was early afternoon before the cloud had lifted enough to see where to go if we wanted to venture higher. I wasn't convinced that the weather would keep improving. But, boredom and the risk of running out of coffee drove me from the tent.

Uphill we went, first tiptoeing through a gulch of stabbing Spaniards—for the uninitiated, imagine a robust, overly assertive flax with particularly sharpened tips—then scuffling across a scree slope of the three-steps-up, one-slide-back kind, and finally skirting around the edge of crumbling snow-ice on the Foster Glacier.

Eventually, we reached the 400-metre-high rock slab that

forms the upper part of Williams. By now, the wind had eased to a cool breeze, most of the fresh snow had melted, and some of the clouds were oozing away. But water runnels still streaked the rock. Even the air felt damp.

I looked at my watch and quickly calculated there wasn't enough time left in the day to attempt the climb.

'Mate, I'm not keen to carry on,' I said. 'I just don't reckon it's worth it.'

'Fair enough,' Jamie replied without so much as a hint of argument. Again, I was surprised at his passivity.

My friend sat on a flat boulder near the edge of the glacier. He studied the mountain for a few minutes. Sunlight reached down through the cloud to settle on a vague arête that was midway up the wall, highlighting the rock's reddish hue. For those few, light-filled moments, the arête and the ramp of rock leading up to it almost looked inviting.

Jamie reached down, picked up a smooth pebble, and cupped it in his hand. Then he glanced at me.

'Do you mind if I go on alone, Paul? I reckon I might try to solo it.'

This was a good idea. Given how little daylight remained, it was probably the only viable option. Soloing would be much quicker than roped climbing. It would also be riskier.

My constant conundrum in the mountains was exposed again, my mind picking over a scab that, even over many years, had never quite healed: *What are the dangers I can't see? How safe do I need to feel today? Is the risk worth it? Do I really want this? Do I believe in myself?*

It was my turn to study the sunlit face again, to try to judge how difficult the climbing might be and whether I was up for the added exposure of ascending without a rope. At the same time, I was trying not to second-guess my earlier decision not to climb. I was attempting to work out the mountain's mood as well as my own.

Jamie was a stronger technical climber than I was. And he would move more quickly over the terrain rising before us, especially without a rope.

I took a deep breath, and told myself I was happy enough to stick with my gut.

'Go for it,' I replied, trying to hide any disappointment in my voice. 'Maybe take one of the ropes and a small rack. Just in case you need to bail and abseil back down, eh?'

'Okay. Sure.'

I could tell that my friend didn't want to carry extra weight in his pack. He had assessed the face and figured he could climb it alone, without the need for protection. I reckon he only took the rope to appease me.

It's an odd experience to sit inactive and safe, partway up the side of a mountain, as a climbing partner and good mate— someone I cared for a great deal—commits himself (or herself) to a risky objective.

Beneath the upper wall of Williams, I felt voyeuristic, detached, and even a little bit guilty for not being with Jamie to share the risk and decision-making with him. I believe that trusting your partner and constantly looking out for each other's well-being are essential parts of competent teamwork in mountaineering. So too is recognising your limitations.

I sat and watched as Jamie cramponed across a tongue of ice towards Mount Williams. He traversed each gaping, blue-black crevasse that descended into the bowels of the Foster Glacier, keeping well clear of their crumbling edges, until he reached the edge of the rock. He prodded at a bulge of glacier that was closest to the wall, checking its stability, searching for a safe place to cross from ice to rock.

Atop a mound of moraine that bridged a gap between the glacier and the huge slab of greywacke above, Jamie paused to remove his crampons and boots. He replaced them with rock shoes. Then he leaned towards the rock. I could see him reach out to put one and then both of his hands upon it. My friend looked to the sky for one final check of what was coming, or perhaps to give thanks. He started to climb.

Jamie moved slowly at first, testing how firmly each flake or nubbin of rock was attached to the mountain before pulling or standing on it. Now more confident with the quality of the greywacke, he easily mantled a short bulge that, from where I sat, looked difficult and exposed—especially without a backup rope and a partner to do the belaying.

Late afternoon sunlight seemed to follow Jamie across and then up the wall, highlighting the redness of the rock as well as his flow with the intricacies of the environment. Everything was as it should be. My friend appeared in control of himself, and of the climb. Composed. At peace.

Jamie paused at a thin edge. He looked back down. Even from a distance, I could see that he was grinning. He waved towards me, then disappeared around the vague arête the sun had been highlighting earlier. The wall became empty again.

I sat for a few more minutes and focussed on the space my friend had just vanished from. I continued to listen for any sound of him moving, all the time wondering of his progress, while still enjoying the warmth and the quiet ambience.

Yes, I was jealous of Jamie. I was annoyed that I hadn't been confident enough in my abilities to take the opportunity as he had. It wasn't the first time I had felt this way in the mountains. But, I tried not to beat myself up too much because I figured—really, I *knew*—that it wouldn't be the last time I would have to deal with such a decision. My relationship with climbing was like agreeing to a never-ending conundrum.

Then I heard something falling. Perhaps it was a boulder, or a chunk of ice broken from the glacier. The thing tumbled and clunked unseen in the shadows, echoes following its progress, a reminder of the space beneath us, and of the gravity that makes that space matter.

The receding echoes reinforced any tension that I felt. Everything in the mountains is in flux. We can never fully relax or be at peace, not in a place like this. Not in *any* place like this. Thinking back now, I was probably naive for not considering that the noise of something falling might have been Jamie. I'd figured he was too good a climber to make a mistake.

Sunlight passed behind a ridge on the other side of the valley. The air cooled. I blew into my cupped hands and rubbed them together. It was time to move. Starting the long scramble back down the scree towards our tent site, I decided on a different route from the way we had ascended, mostly to avoid the valley of attacking Spaniards but also so I could get a look at the lower part of Williams that had so far been concealed beneath the Foster Glacier.

Even as I drew closer to it, the lower cirque of rock tried to remain hidden in the late afternoon shadows. A swirl of wind sent ripples over a small tarn at the base of the wall, before the water smoothed again with the returning stillness. I picked up a flat stone and skimmed it across the tarn. Skipping stones was something I'd used to do as a kid at the beach. *One...two... three...four...* I counted before the stone lost momentum and sunk into the void with one final, defiant *plop*.

The stone-skipping was an act intended, even if subconsciously, to try to relieve the tension of being there. In certain moods—either the mountain's or my own—I find that a setting such as this can feel eerie and unnerving. It's as if the earth is holding its breath until I have passed by. There are no obvious signs of life, other than the odd tahr scrambling along a distant ridge line, or perhaps the world's only mountain parrot, the kea, calling out as it circles overhead. This is a place to visit, perhaps discover a feature enticing enough to want to climb, but then to leave again. Thinking back now, I guess part of my mood was feeling like I had deserted Jamie.

The lower wall of Williams was mirrored by the tarn. I enjoyed the seeming incongruence of the reflection, how small it seemed to the reality of what rose before me. After finding a flattish boulder to sit on, I took my pack off to ferret inside it. I walked back to the tarn to refill my water bottle, and the water was so cold it made me gasp after each mouthful.

I needed perspective. *What am I looking at?* So, I spread a map open. I studied it, and then the landscape above. *Yes!* The rock had features that might be of interest. There were gullies where ice threatened to fall and would be funnelled from above, but there were also rounded buttresses that appeared safe, or safe enough. Perhaps they could be reached. Perhaps they were fractured enough from the cold so as to allow for pieces of protection to be inserted.

The wall was aesthetically pleasing. It curved in one long arch, like the inside of a coliseum. Mostly, the rock looked smooth, worn from decades of glacial movement. In places, it rose like a giant gladiator's staircase towards the Foster that waited and groaned, as a crowd might, hundreds of metres above.

Could there be a way to link the whole route, starting next to the tarn and climbing right to the summit? I tried to connect the various aspects of the wall that I could see, imagining where I thought the cruxes might be: a short bulge here; a blank section there; a hidden gully that might or might not join to the next ledge. Perhaps the entire wall *could* be climbed.

I started to develop a plan, an inkling to return to this quiet place to try again. But any attempt would have to keep for another time. Storing what I had studied in my memory, I stood up, reset my pack, and continued down the valley to our campsite.

It took Jamie barely an hour to solo the upper slab of Williams. He was back at the tent only an hour and a half behind me. I spotted him descending through the Spaniards, moving as efficiently and tirelessly as ever, like he was on a wander to the local shop.

My friend had an aura of contentment that can form after such a climb. It made me feel jealous again. I cursed my lack of commitment but then tried to soothe the inevitable self-flagellation by reinforcing my reasons why I hadn't done as he had. *Trust your judgement, Paul. Believe in yourself. There will be another opportunity.*

Despite what almost felt like an internal diatribe, I was still happy for Jamie. From what I had seen, he'd climbed the route as competently and as safely as possible. And, after such a quick ascent, he didn't even look tired.

Fit bastard, I thought as I handed him a hot drink.

Then I made a point of asking: '*Jeez*, mate. What took you so long?'

TWO

As is the way of nature versus nurture, a love for the mountains is something certain people are either born with or grow into. For me, it was the latter.

While living in Christchurch and pretending to study at Lincoln University, I ventured into the South Island's mountainous interior as often as possible. Weekends and exam breaks were usually spent bouldering at Castle Hill, rock climbing on the Port Hills overlooking the city, or mountain climbing in Arthur's Pass National Park.

In 1994, I succeeded in reaching the summit of Aoraki / Mount Cook. I stood on the highest point of New Zealand and scanned a horizon dominated to the west by the denim-blue sweep of the Tasman Sea. But it was the sea of mountains that focused my attention. Seemingly endless snow summits protruded, like beacons of light, from the valley cloud. It felt like each one was signalling me. Over the following decades, I attempted to respond to their call.

Memories of mountains now flow through much of my life. These memories are filled with good mates and hard-earned adventures. They are special moments, like watching Jamie on Mount Williams, or trying to mimic his contortions on an unlikely chandelier of ice in nearby South Temple Valley; soloing with another friend, Kynan Bazley, up a fin of rock that rose over a kilometre high on Mount Hopkins; exploring as many alpine corners as could be found with my longtime climbing partner, Mat Woods; and following my wife Shelley's footprints in the snow up unclimbed mountains in Nepal and India.

Not only have mountains provided me with an opportunity to test myself, but they have also allowed me to feel a strong sense of place and of being. I am drawn to them because of what lies within as much as what lies in front of, or, more accurately, *above* me. As New Zealand poet John Newton once wrote, mountains 'are a story you tell about yourself, a story you are journeying into, which swallows you.'

So obvious in dominating our physical landscape, mountains have the potential to also dominate the landscape of our minds. They evolve into a psychological presence so indisputable—for some, so necessary—that everything else fades to a blur of mundane unimportance. Life without them remains too predictable. Too boring. We become focussed solely on the next trip.

The defiance of such physical and mental barriers is significant to the attraction. Sometimes, the mountains I am drawn to remain impenetrable, but they carry with that impenetrability a suggestion of *perhaps one day*. Other mountains stimulate thoughts of beauty and desire in my mind even when I am not near them. Not surprisingly, they become inspirational.

More often than not, the mountains I am attracted to will instil doubt. A certain mountain might keep me awake at night, especially if I am camped beneath its shadow or in the aftermath of a previous epic encounter with it. The knowledge of its existence encourages me to try harder, to discover, and hopefully become, a better version of myself.

Mountains have made me laugh and cry. While among them, I have been physically at my best and mentally at my worst. I have made good decisions and bad, and I have been both relieved and horrified at the results. While climbing, fatigue and discomfort have become constant, almost reassuring companions. At times, fear has almost overwhelmed my ability to move or even think. I have been close to death in the mountains, but not always while being afraid of what I am facing. I have also been incredibly lucky, and I am extremely grateful for that.

Climbing for more than thirty years has taught me many things, including that committing to certain mountains carries a price. Summits not reached have made me recognise and then try to understand what I might lack inside—that cold stab of doubt that always finds me at my weakest. But, being at my weakest is also when I am likely to learn the most. Too much success breeds hubris and complacency.

Mountains have forced me to cope with extreme adversity, and occasionally, with the hammer blow of a sudden, heart-shattering loss. And, perhaps at their most elemental, mountains have made me question: *what is the true worth of an act done or not done?*

Many decades ago, my grandfather purchased an oil painting from the Wellington artist Nugent Welch. Welch was considered New Zealand's first official war artist, and, after the end of World War I, he turned his attention to painting landscapes. The artwork my grandfather bought was a recreation of the Mackenzie Basin in the heart of the South Island. Welch chose to ignore the milky blue lakes the region is perhaps most visually renowned for. Instead, he focused on a cloud-smeared sky, a sunburned land, and a distant horizon of mountains.

In the foreground, a rough track shows the way, illustrating that it is possible to travel through such hard country. The viewer's eyes and mind are drawn into the scene, encouraged to consider where the trail might take them if they are adventurous enough. In the background, the mountains wait aloof and distant.

As a child, I would sit on the floor of my grandparents' house to study the environment that Welch had captured so vividly. It seemed such a dry and barren landscape, especially in comparison to the heavily forested, humid countryside I was familiar with growing up in the northern-most part of New Zealand. I tried to imagine what such a place would be like to experience and explore.

Along with the painting, my grandfather had purchased books about the exploits of high-altitude climbers. These were among my earliest exposures to mountains. I spent hours reading in my grandfather's library. It was easy to become lost in the novels of Mark Twain, Joseph Conrad, Robert Louis Stevenson, H.G. Wells, Charles Dickens, and others—for good reason. I find there is a natural connection between colonial adventure literature and mountaineering. And, although my grandfather didn't seem remotely interested in climbing, he still collected books about great alpine and ice exploration. The first mountaineering book I read was *The Ascent of Everest* by John Hunt. *Alpine Tragedy* by Charles Gos was the second, and Graeme Dingle's *Wall of Shadows* was the third.

Perhaps it was inevitable that mountain literature and imagery ensnared my young mind. That painting and those stories helped spark my imagination, which later led to a desire for adventures well beyond what I had already experienced of the sea and the landscape near home. To an impressionable young mind with an infinitely long life stretching ahead, risking it all in some unknown, high place seemed wonderfully rebellious.

Welch's painting now hangs from a wall in my home, and those mountains within it have shaped much of my life. My grandfather's copies of *The Ascent of Everest* and *Alpine Tragedy* are also on my bookshelf (but I recently needed to purchase another copy of *Wall of Shadows*).

Sitting here now and writing these words, I can stop for a few moments to look up at Welch's artwork. Despite the paint flaking and the picture frame being well past its prime, it is still easy to imagine myself within the scene that he recreated. I close my eyes to work and life. I follow the trail.

This shift in perspective declutters my mind. Without effort, I find myself listening for a stream gurgling nearby, and for birds chattering about the coming day. I imagine the coolness of a morning breeze against my skin. I wait for the first light to warm my fingers and toes. All the time I am breathing, slowly, in through my nose then out through my mouth. I open my eyes again, but only when I am ready.

I have spent years exploring the mountains that Welch had

painted long before I was born, traversing the edges of what is known as 'big sky country', the land that makes up the Mackenzie Basin.

Perhaps my favourite escape is to recall—or better yet, visit—two particular valleys leading north from a lake. From downcountry, they appear broad, flat-floored, and initially sparse with vegetation. Their rivers are stony and braided. Sheep and cattle graze their grassy banks and lower terraces. On busier weekends, four-wheel-drive enthusiasts invade the quietude. They bounce over every hill and dale, one or more likely to get stuck while trying to plough his or her own route between the spaced huts. But traveling on foot, going both farther and higher, an opportunity exists for a different, much more engaging experience. An opportunity exists to embrace the quiet moments.

In my mind, I am standing at the southern edge of the lake and looking north. The valley to the right is the Dobson. It is almost arrow straight, drawing a line towards the midday sun. One can easily see what adventures await within its twin, alpine backbones. Most of the highest mountains are gathered at the farthest end of the valley, seemingly paying homage to their cloud-piercing talisman, Aoraki / Mount Cook, on the distant skyline.

The valley to the left, the Hopkins, carries a more subtle, right-leaning curve. What's to come is not revealed unless one chooses to enter. The mountains here are more spread. Summits seem to have their own breathing space. Pleated skirts of deep-green forest lead to rocky ridges and sharp-edged summits—discoveries waiting to be unveiled.

I first visited the Hopkins Valley in the winter of 1989. I started walking up the valley from a narrow gravel road that ended beneath the eastern slopes of a mountain I would later become familiar with—Rabbiters Peak. The air was brisk. There were patches of old, hard snow on the valley floor that crunched noisily beneath my boots. My fingers grew numb inside my gloves and my breath clouded before me. Despite the cold, I was keen to explore.

By chance, I stumbled upon a track near Monument Hut. Following it through what I found to be a strangely open beech forest—especially when considering the cloying denseness of Northland's rainforests—I crossed a swing bridge over where the Huxley River pinched and grew turbulent. Not knowing where I was going didn't seem to matter. I felt inquisitive, invigorated, and at peace.

Finally, I reached a clearing in the trees where I could look out—*up*—at the snow-wrapped summits. The mountains closest seemed to bend over me. Their presence felt overpowering, as if there was no option at that moment to be aware of anything else. Other mountains across the valley seemed to draw away mysteriously. Their summits remained hidden beyond walls and ridges.

I didn't know what to think. Even scanning all around, trying to piece together different parts of the landscape to get a sense of scale, provided little understanding of what might exist up there. Yet, the very highest points beckoned me. I tried to make sense of the words I had read in my grandfather's mountain books and how they related to the landscape I was now witnessing.

Not everything about the landscape felt alluring. The tangata whenua, the first people of the land, rightly named this area Ōhau, or Place of Wind. The northwesterly wind at its most powerful here is an affront to the senses. It beats you like a warning: *Turn around!* It buffers your clothing. It makes even breathing difficult. Each step against it requires effort. All the time, your mind doubts the sanity of continuing. *What is this place?* But turn your back and you can gallop downwind to the lowlands, like riding a stallion to safety.

The wind increased that day in the winter of '89. Beech trees around me swayed and groaned like old men, and the summits gathered strange-looking, upside-down saucers of cloud. Even though I was relatively inexperienced with backcountry travel, I had enough sense to recognise that it was time to start heading back down the valley to my vehicle.

My initial experience of walking up the Hopkins Valley and staring at those strange summits was little different from studying Welch's painting or reading those first mountaineering books. *What do the words mean? What am I even looking at?* I may have been out hiking before, but I had just been looking, not *seeing*. I wasn't yet capable of understanding the depth of the experience.

I had no real knowledge of mountains and no idea of what I was gazing up at or how to engage with something so all-encompassing. There was too much landscape to take in. There were too many things to consider. And the only way to begin to understand was to go up.

Of course, my musings were all theoretical. No one else in my family climbed, and the notion of mountaineering in the cold unknown of the Deep South was about as far away and foreign from Northland's sunny beaches, and warm-water waves surfing in board shorts, as I could get.

I was certainly intrigued. There was an unsettling tingle in my gut that I hadn't felt before. I couldn't work out whether it was a good or a bad thing, but that was part of the attraction. The more I thought about mountains, the more I wanted to find out about them.

Two decades later, I had the good fortune of meeting Jamie Vinton-Boot. Shelley and I had just recently moved north from Dunedin to Christchurch, and I was scheduled to give a talk in the Garden City to local members of the New Zealand Alpine Club.

At the meeting, I spoke about my passion for unclimbed routes in some of the lesser-known mountainous areas, in particular espousing the benefits of pursuing 'weekend smash-and-grab missions' into the Hopkins and its surrounding valleys. With the bravado of a used car salesman, I hinted at huge slabs of undiscovered rock in summer and long streaks of ice hidden in the coldest valleys in winter.

Most of the audience sat and listened politely. They gazed at my photos of recent adventures and then of the ridges and rock faces that were inspiring me to explore further. Although they nodded as if they understood, they didn't say anything.

But, there was one young man near the back of the room who kept asking questions. Lots of questions. He was standing off to one side of the main group of seated listeners. I noticed his lean physique and overdeveloped arms, his quiet voice, and the intensity of his stare. It seemed that he was giving each question plenty of consideration before asking it. At times, he had the slightest stutter while trying to come up with the right words.

After the meeting ended, the young man walked up to Shelley and me to talk further. He put his hand out, quite formally, and introduced himself, and I recognised his name from climbing reports in the Alpine Club magazine.

Jamie seemed shy, but his grin would widen whenever the conversation centred on mountains. I figured that he probably climbed quite a few grades harder than I did, so I was surprised when he asked whether we might go on a trip together.

The start of our climbing partnership actually involved a lot of surfing. But, once the weather sorted itself out, Jamie and I got our groove on in the mountains. There was a sixteen-year difference in our ages—a young punk who breezed uphill without sweating, replying to inquiries about whether we were following a track with 'I am the track!', partnering with an almost-has-been prone to finding scenic locations to rest and 'take in the ambience'. I had an eye for new lines and a well-developed sense of self-preservation, and Jamie had enough enthusiasm and upwards momentum for the both of us.

I quickly realised that my new, much younger friend had an unfortunate physiology, or unfortunate for those who wanted to go climbing with him. There's fit, and then there's *fit!*

'I don't know what it is, but I don't really get tired,' Jamie felt the need to mention during one of our early trips together, while I struggled to keep pace with him. Not enough oxygen was reaching my brain to come up with a suitably witty or sarcastic reply. Eventually, I slumped to the ground, mumbling an excuse about needing to retighten the laces on my boots.

'It's funny because I was such a skinny kid at school,' he continued, politely ignoring my sudden semi-collapse. 'I was really good at aerobic activities like running and swimming, but I hated team sports. Girls didn't notice me at all.'

And then Jamie had discovered climbing. 'Someone told me that if I wanted to be a good climber, I had to do lots of pull-ups,' he said. 'So I did. It didn't help my climbing technique much, but within six months, I grew muscles.'

'I bet that improved your chances with the girls,' I managed to reply after my breathing had returned to normal.

Jamie laughed. 'Actually, no, it didn't. I'd go to parties but the wrong type of girls would come up and start touching me. I didn't know what to do. Getting muscles only made things worse. In the end, I didn't even want to go to my senior dance. I just went climbing instead.'

Jamie had since recovered from those awkward beginnings, both on the climbing and girlfriend front, but he still reputedly did lots of pull-ups. I'd noticed a well-worn campus board fixed over the inside kitchen door of the house that he and his partner Jess McLachlan had recently purchased.

Even by climbing standards, Jamie's arms always remained particularly well-developed.

Over the following months, our climbing partnership—as well as our friendship—strengthened. I introduced Jamie to the mountains of the Hopkins, especially some of the more difficult lines I was hoping to attempt but doubted whether I had the skills to climb at the time. We grew to appreciate each other's company, and I realised that Jamie shared my passion for exploration and adventure in lots of different parts of New Zealand, rather than just focussing on the well-known areas like most of the stronger climbers tended to do.

Teaming up with one of the best all-round climbers in the country made me all the more aware of my age, self-noted weaknesses, and varying levels of motivation. I understood that I would have to train harder if I wanted to keep up with Jamie. On each new climb, I found myself being pushed further and further outside of my comfort zone. I had to learn to manage my doubts and my fear. My tendency of being overly cautious was constantly challenged by Jamie's go-for-it attitude.

However, our team dynamic also highlighted my strengths in the mountains. I had a knack for understanding a particular environment, and for finding quality rock and ice within it. And my conservative decision-making was an added safety buffer whenever we ventured somewhere new, or when the weather or climbing conditions were more unpredictable.

If I discovered a worthwhile project, no doubt Jamie could get us up the hardest bits, and I could get us home.

THREE

One of my grandfather's mountaineering books—*Wall of Shadows,* by Graeme Dingle—was about the 1975 New Zealand climbers' expedition to attempt the north face of Jannu in Nepal. Included in the photos from Dingle's trip were two images of a beautiful, aesthetic, unclimbed mountain the Kiwi climbers called the 'White Wave'. Known by the Nepalese as Anidesha Chuli, the mountain was right next to Jannu. Decades after that expedition, those photos from Dingle's book encouraged another two Antipodean expeditions to that remote area of Nepal to try to climb Anidesha Chuli. The second expedition, in 2014, was mine.

The paths we choose versus the paths that are chosen for us—perhaps a few words in an old book is all it takes. Or a single, grainy photograph. Unexpected contours on a map. Blank spaces in a guidebook. Whatever the instigation, an inkling is formed, creating the first stage of desire. Knowledge waits to be gained in some unknown place.

A climbing friend once asked me why I was so keen to search for new lines in the mountains. Surely, they reasoned, it would be better to climb the best routes that had been done before. To focus on the 'classics'. Climbing was tough enough without adding to the challenge. And by trying something new—something unknown—I was increasing the chances of the climb not being worthwhile.

Uncertainty. Striving for what might not even exist. How can I measure the worth of that? Or of any climbing? Deciding to take on a climb isn't like deciding whether to go to surfing at the beach or to a cafe or to a movie cinema for the afternoon. Much more is at stake. Along with the likelihood and the consequence of risk, there is always a chance that the climb may be my last.

So, I look backwards to move forwards. I try to learn from my mistakes and near misses, as well as from the experiences, mistakes, and perspectives of others. This better prepares me to make more considered decisions. Or, at least, I hope it does.

The most obvious question is *why*? Non-climbers have asked me this many times over the years, in various social settings, with varying degrees of voyeuristic interest and, sometimes, even incredulity. Why have I chosen to commit to something that most sane people consider a pointless, or even reckless, endeavour? When there are so many other experiences potentially just as engaging—not to mention, safer—to try, why decide to go *climbing*?

I accept that this is a fair question. And, depending on how it is framed, it is a question not always easy to articulate a reasonable answer for. French alpinist Lionel Terray hit the nail squarely on its head with the title of one of his climbing books: *Conquistadors of the Useless*.

While plenty of climbers I know and respect don't give the question of *why?* too much thought, I have tried to unravel this quandary over the passing seasons. I suppose it has been for my own benefit as much as anyone else's.

Author Barry Lopez once wrote that 'One of the great dreams of man must be to find some place between the extremes of nature and civilisation where it is possible to live without regret.' Otherwise, our increasingly heavy footprint upon the earth will continue to take us further and further away from connecting with it, fully acknowledging it and, ultimately, having the desire or ability to save it. We need experience to be able to relate. We need hardship to appreciate. We need understanding to care.

But connecting with nature is only the starting point towards my understanding of why I choose to climb. And then a single, earth-shattering experience changes everything. The various motivations and justifications I have established in my mind vanish in less time than it takes for me to inhale a single, deep, searing breath. When you commit everything, that is exactly what you risk losing.

To build an understanding, perhaps it is simplest to begin with the framework, with what we can *see*. As climbing author David Craig observed, crags and mountains 'act on us as the moon does on the seas, inert mineral masses exerting their force, leading us to their poles'. Craig's analogy suggests there is a certain inevitability to the relationship that forms between climber and mountain. Perhaps we don't need to cognitively understand the relationship. It is going to develop regardless.

Or, at the other extreme, take early explorer George Mallory's much-quoted and seemingly throwaway response to why he wanted to be the first person to climb the world's highest mountain, Mount Everest, on the border of Nepal and China. 'Because it's there,' he simply said. To me, this smacks of arrogance, or at least of a lack of patience in trying to help others understand. What I believe Mallory was really saying is: 'You have no idea because you're not a climber, and I don't particularly care to explain.'

As a counter to Mallory's attitude, it's fair to acknowledge that the mountains aren't any more special than other natural wonders. The sea can be just as marvellous, and not nearly so dangerous depending on how you choose to interact with it. Therefore, it is important to acknowledge that a climber's insistence on tackling dangerous peaks, when equally beautiful, safer adventures are available elsewhere, might seem unreasonable to some.

With any environment, there is—or should be—awe in simply observing the existence of our natural world: what has been created through the meeting of land and water, moulded by tectonic thrust and erosion, harassed by weather, nurtured by air, covered by growing things in summer and perhaps the weight of snow in winter.

Moving with Shelley to Christchurch in 2009, with its view of the Southern Alps—Kā Tiritiri o te Moana—was a constant reminder that we lived in a country of mountains. Along with the ocean, they are our greatest and most obvious geological barriers. Their slopes are filled with stories, legend, and folklore. To see them, one only needs to look out the window. Their presence becomes familiar. They provide recognition, and the reassurance, that we are home.

For me, it is comforting to have a gentle or jagged rise somewhere on the horizon, summits shimmering with light on a clear morning, or gathering a frown of clouds as another storm approaches. The presence of these broken castles soothes me. Welch's painting, it seems, has become permanently etched into my psyche.

When compared to most of the world's landmasses, New Zealand is considered a mountainous country. Each region of Aotearoa has its prominent high points, its beacons, its protectors. Mountains have always been significant to the people of this land. Rising sharply towards Ranginui, the Sky Father, mountains watched over the Māori world long before the arrival of the Pākehā. Summits were considered places of great awe, and they carried a spiritual presence. Nearly every range and prominent peak in the country is linked to local tribal identity.

Stories were imagined to explain the landscape. According to Māori folklore, there once gathered many mountains in the Central Plateau region of the North Island. It is said that Taranaki, Tongariro, Ngāuruhoe, Ruapehu, Pūtauaki, and Tauhara all competed for the attention of the bush-clad Pihanga. Tongariro, the dominant mountain, and the next strongest, Taranaki, fought most often. Fires would burn from their summits and smoke would cloud the sky. In one battle, Tongariro lost his head, which fell into Lake Taupō and can still be seen as Motutaiko Island, while Taranaki received a blow that took a chunk from his side.

Eventually, Tongariro defeated Taranaki, banishing him and the other mountains. Putauaki travelled north to the edge of the Kaingaroa Plains, while Tauhara moved east as far as Lake Taupō. But Taranaki, whose love for Pihanga was said to be the strongest, ventured the farthest, gouging a channel through the landscape that became the Whanganui River. He followed the setting sun as far as he could, to the edge of the island, where he now remains.

Bad weather indicates Taranaki is weeping for his loss of Pihanga, while Tongariro and Ngāuruhoe display their continuing anger towards him with occasional plumes of smoke and lava. Taranaki may one day return for Pihanga. Some consider it unwise to live along the path between them.

Stories told of mountains are a way to explain geological individuality; all tend to have some human element or humans involved in the mountain's existence. It is natural to personify mountains. We understand them—or try to understand them—because we want to interact, to be immersed in their presence.

The craggy outline of Mount Manaia in Northland was perhaps the maunga I most identified with in my youth. While only a shadow of the much more dominating mountains further south, my brothers Glen, Steve, and I still loved to scramble up its exposed rocky flanks to reach the trig at the summit. There, we would gaze over the blue expanse of the Pacific Ocean, wondering about what we had just experienced and where our lives might take us.

Mount Hikurangi—a summit near East Cape that is sacred to the Ngāti Porou iwi—is the first place on New Zealand's mainland to be roused awake by the sun. During the one time I climbed it, a lone magpie took a particular disliking to my pack and head. 'Value this place or I'll teach you a lesson,' the feisty guard-bird seemed to be telling me in no uncertain terms.

Further west, the forested slopes of Pirongia Mountain were believed to be home to the patupaiarehe, a mythical people with fair skin, green eyes, and red hair. Perhaps the story originated among local Māori because of a few early Scottish castaways. No doubt, whoever resided there would have felt connected with the environment, and treasured its secret corridors of travel. When I visited Glen and Steve, who lived in the nearby city of Hamilton, we raced up the mountain's modern corridors till our lungs threatened to burst or we reached the summit of Pirongia, whichever came first.

While the mountains on the North Island are generally more spread apart, and not very difficult to climb, the South Island is a different story. Great clusters of them dominate the landscape, the most notable being the Southern Alps, which stretches 500 kilometres—almost the length of the island.

Towers of greywacke, schist, granite, and limestone form a seemingly impenetrable barrier between the South Island's eastern and western sides. Summits influence weather and surrounding vegetation. In only a few places have the Southern Alps been breached for vehicle access, making for a dramatic, scenic, and somewhat tenuous passage in the company of giants. Passing so close, the physical presence of the mountains can be more fully appreciated.

Thinking about the mountains in Welch's painting, and then about trying to place myself in the feeling of that environment, leads me to conclude that everything we see and experience is also a reflection of time. Just as we have our own fleeting, personal experiences, landscapes also go through a lifespan. Snow-covered summits might appear like teeth against the gaping blue of the sky, but by the end of each summer, most of the snow has melted. Rocky mountains seem like the impenetrable walls of a castle, but their defences are still able to be defeated, crumbling piece by piece over time or in a great rush during a landslide or an earthquake.

What do climbers see when they look at mountains? Not just huge, natural monoliths to be held in awe, justified by stories or perhaps feared. Not just a massif of rock and ice, or something that seems a foreign landscape.

Climbers try to understand the various features on mountains, eyeing potential routes up them—the lines to climb. A ridge is not just a ridge, a gully not simply a gully. These become places for opportunity, for challenge, and for what I like to refer to as treasured pathways.

For me, there is the added quandary of looking at mountains and trying to describe what I see, and then also how that makes me feel. Considering this now has me recalling a quote by surf journalist Mike McGinty on the difficulty of capturing the essence of his sport, which I think is equally applicable to climbing. McGinty writes: 'I don't need paper and ink...I need elongated vowel sounds and exaggerated hand movements. Can you feel it? Did it work? Do you have any idea what surfing is really like? Sure. But only because you're a surfer. Not because I said so.'

Like surfers, climbers need to do more than just look. We have to approach what we see, find a way to introduce ourselves. We need to connect. We might become immersed and, hopefully for a time, lost as we journey through a landscape of contrasting moods. A landscape with the potential for creating our own treasured pathway. A landscape that challenges us, which might choose to swallow us or, at the very least, change us for the better.

FOUR

If mountains are the *where*, then it is also necessary to decipher the *what*—the act of climbing them. The fundamentals of movement, using two hands and two feet, of moving *up*. It seems a natural thing to want to do. We did it as monkeys, and easily enough as children.

Put something in front of my brothers and me—a high fence, a building, a tree, anything that blocked our path—and no doubt as kids we would have attempted to get up it. There were times the three of us raced to be first to the top. Other times—like when we discovered a steep wall of volcanic conglomerate on the eastern flank of Manaia—we helped each other, so we could all get up together. My brothers were my first climbing partners; they were taller than me and more athletic, but we each had our strengths. Even as youngsters, we already understood the importance of teamwork.

Climbing seemed normal to us then, a thing just done

and not something to consider so deeply—certainly not like I am trying to do now. In my youth, I had a knack for finding adventures for the three of us and for any of our friends who were game enough to tag along. 'Shortcuts home', I used to call them, even when they usually took much longer than the normal route. One shortcut involved lunging from crumbly rock partway up a coastal cliff to an exposed pōhutukawa tree root, legs dangling in space amid the sudden sour taste in our mouths and the surge of strength that comes with unexpected fear. I can still clearly remember the look on Glen's face: *Shit! Well, we're in it now. Only one way out.*

Eventually, we accepted that my attempted shortcuts could be—and usually *were*—anything but. The knowledge didn't deter us. Of course, as children and teenagers, we didn't have much of an understanding of consequence. We would dare each other to give stuff a go. Little more than our enthusiasm, intent, and overconfidence kept us safe. Our self-belief shielded us from reality.

But then Steve, my youngest brother, fell off a jungle gym at his school and broke his arm. Later, I broke my nose (although this was while playing cricket rather than climbing). We began to realise that perhaps we weren't bulletproof; there could be a negative outcome to our adventuring.

Despite a growing realisation, the three of us continued to ignore the idea of something going wrong for as long as we could. Like all good youth, we turned up the volume and rebelled against the inevitable.

It turned out that climbing wasn't the only thing Jamie

excelled at; his partner, Jess, once referred to him as 'The Bread Whisperer'. For Jamie, flour plus water equalled magic. He had been exclusively making his own bread for about six years by the time we met. Around twelve months into the obsession, he collected some grapes from a friend's house so that he could establish his own sourdough starter rather than keep using someone else's. Starting from scratch and using locally sourced ingredients were important to Jamie.

Jamie and Jess's bread-and-pizza nights became legendary in their neighbourhood, as well as the wider Christchurch climbing community. Dinner at their home was also a good place for Shelley and me to immerse ourselves in the local climbing fraternity. Sometimes there would be quite a gathering, everyone telling tall stories and getting amped for the next adventure; other times it was just Jamie, Jess, and us.

One evening, over Jamie's bread and a second bottle of wine, the conversation, not surprisingly, turned towards climbing.

'I was super fit as a kid, a bit of a mountain goat in terms of my stamina,' Jamie proclaimed, a glass of wine in one hand and a slight furrow of his eyebrows as he recalled his childhood.

'Maybe you are part goat,' I quipped. 'That *would* explain a lot.'

I was interested to learn how Jamie's taste for adventures in his youth compared to my own. Growing up in Wellington, Jamie said he got into tramping through high school. He started venturing into the nearby Tararua Ranges with schoolmates. Then he talked about not enjoying the conventional structure of team sports at school, and having a lack of confidence in big groups of people.

Instead, Jamie revelled in the freedom that came with long days tramping in the hills, and of 'not knowing what was around the next corner'.

Listening to Jamie, I got a feeling that I'd heard this story before. Jamie's early life experiences were strikingly similar to that of Graeme Dingle.

Jamie laughed when I suggested this.

'Dingle's book was one of the first mountaineering books I read,' he admitted. 'I identified with what he'd gone through, and the kinds of things that he'd tried to do as a youngster. Like trying to run the length of the Tararuas in a day, or doing really long traverses of the range. I started to set challenges like that for myself. I just had this burning desire to push myself, to get as high or go as far as I could.'

A new indoor rock climbing wall was built just down the road from Jamie's high school in Lower Hutt. Rock climbing became another way to improve his skills.

'Mountaineering, or as close as I could get to it in the Tararuas, was my thing; I knew that,' Jamie explained. 'But obviously, I couldn't get into the hills every day, so rock climbing became a natural progression. Pretty soon, I was bouldering or rope climbing almost every night.'

The final summer of his seventh form year at school, Jamie and three friends travelled down to Mount Cook Village for a go at 'real mountains'. Jamie remembered driving along Mount Cook Road into the village and seeing huge avalanches peel off the ice cliffs on Mount Sefton.

'It was a bit different to the Tararuas,' he said with a wry grin. 'I was bewildered and excited at the same time. I looked up, wondering how to be able to climb anything like that, but knowing that I wanted to.'

Jamie recalled the tick list for the trip being 'somewhat ambitious'. Probably fortuitously, bad weather prevented the inexperienced group from climbing much at all. But the following Easter, after enrolling at Lincoln University in

Christchurch, Jamie returned to Mount Cook with good friend Thomas Adamson. They managed to climb both the Footstool and Mount Sealy.

'That set the way forward,' Jamie explained. 'Thomas and I had such a great trip, and we both found the peaks pretty easy. I just knew then that mountaineering was something I had to do. It was so engaging physically and spiritually, making me focus on the moment. It was a fantastic feeling.'

Jamie became more expressive while he spoke, his hands moving as he remembered certain holds or climbing sequences, and his face then spreading into a wide grin. 'I loved the challenge of having to keep it together,' he said, 'of not having interference from everyday life. There was a totality to the experience. I've never found anything else in life that did that to me.'

While studying at Lincoln, Jamie moved into a flat in Christchurch with local rock climbers Derek Thatcher and Ivan Vostinar. What followed was a rather intense sidetrack into hard bouldering and rock climbing. Flatting and training with two of the country's top rock jocks elevated Jamie's ability in technical climbing to a new level.

'Yeah, it was a good time,' he recalled. 'I was lucky to have a couple of mentors like that, but in my heart, it was still mountaineering that I wanted to do. Rock climbing just filled the time when I couldn't go into the mountains.'

Jamie started to focus on taking his new technical skills into the mountains. 'I guess I'm restless in everyday life,' he admitted. 'I always want to be doing something. I can't just sit around and relax. That's why climbing is perfect for me; it's completely absorbing. I figure that it's my religion. When I get into the mountains, everything becomes clear and simple. Climbing gives me a better respect for life and nature, and what it means to be human.'

Jamie's partner Jess was sitting on the sofa, listening to him explain his passion for life and how much climbing affected him. In contrast to Jamie's more reserved nature, Jess is bubbly and engaging. An avid dancer, she felt the need to interrupt Jamie's description of why he enjoyed climbing so much.

'It's not just climbing that provides so much passion,' Jess said. 'I feel like that with my dancing, too.'

We all then discussed 'being in the zone' in various pursuits and how or if 'the zone' differed depending on the level of risk involved. I considered my best moments climbing versus, say, surfing, or playing on a football field. While there seemed little comparison between football and mountaineering, I could see a similarity between paddling into a large wave and the crux of a climbing route. Both required a decision to be made beforehand, followed by absolute commitment, and an acceptance of whatever the outcome would be. There had to be a letting go. And, in that moment of letting go, there rose the potential to reach a certain state of mind. An elusive feeling— even now, I have never lost a craving for it.

Our discussion was becoming rather intense, so I took a break and headed for the toilet. There, I got sidetracked by a stool chart on the wall, along with puzzling over how to flick the light switch on without disturbing two little Lego guys who were doing the wild thing on it. Then I started to read a newspaper cutout that had been stuck to the wall about Jamie and his friend rock-climbing. The story focussed on an eight-metre ground fall Jamie's mate, Troy Mattingley, had taken while leading at The Tors, one of the crags in the Port Hills which overlooked Christchurch. Troy had been badly injured in the fall.

'For a while, I felt responsible for the fall because I put Troy in that position,' Jamie admitted when I later asked him about the accident. 'I was encouraging him from the ground. Maybe we should have done more pre-inspection of the route, to work out where the best holds were. Or, it should have been me that was up there instead of Troy. I was always the one going for it.'

'Did the accident affect your own climbing afterwards?' I asked.

Jamie glanced towards Jess before answering the question. 'It didn't stop me from climbing, but I certainly slowed down for a while. Maybe the whole thing was a timely wake-up call. It was around that time I took up surfing.'

It's fair to say that Jamie's surfing ability didn't quite match that of his climbing. But in both, he exhibited the same go-for-it attitude, even when paddling into double-overhead closeout waves at the city's best surf break, Taylor's Mistake. Despite any whitewater beatings, he normally surfaced with a smile. Not that any inability on a surfboard would have worried Jamie; climbing was his primary goal.

'My passion is to climb technical routes up high, both hard rock and ice, in the mountains,' he said. 'I'd like to free The Mutant on Mount Lendenfeld, maybe repeat Bill and Ted's (a very difficult and rarely formed-up ice route on La Perouse) if it ever forms up again. Those types of harder climbs are inspiring.'

Jamie had been staring into space as he'd spoken. Then he turned to look at me. 'More recently, I guess I've also started to get passionate about exploring new places, finding wee gems of climbs where no one expects them to be,' he said. 'There's always a real adventure getting there, and full commitment's required to climb those types of routes.'

Then, it was Jamie's turn to ask me a question: 'Why do you only climb in the Hopkins area?'

My voice may have come across as a little high-pitched when I quickly, and possibly defensively, replied: 'I've climbed in other areas, too.'

'Well, let's find some cool stuff somewhere else, and we'll go climb it then,' he said.

'Fine,' I replied. 'I will.'

Jamie's observation and slight dig were probably fair enough. My familiarity with the Hopkins had become too much of a reassurance, like returning to a second home. I understood what the challenges were in getting to and then tackling most of the climbs. I knew where to find water, and where the decent clearings existed for pitching a tent or laying out a bivouac bag. The familiarity of it all made me feel safe, or safe enough.

Jamie helped me realise that it was probably time to explore other areas, other mountains. Call his encouragement an opportunity for personal growth, or simply a further push into the unknown—both were part of the reason I took up climbing in the first place. They were continuing lessons throughout my climbing experience, and indeed all of my personal endeavours. *Keep trying new things. Embrace whatever unsettles you. Never be satisfied.*

Then Jamie mentioned that he'd also like to try an overseas expedition in the next year or two, 'not necessarily on a big, well-known peak, but something technical, maybe over 6000 metres in India or Pakistan'.

'Altitude is the great leveller,' I replied, thinking about my own trips to the Greater Ranges overseas, and how the added height had affected my ability and confidence. 'You never know how much it's going to knock you around. And one trip can be totally different from the next.'

Jamie nodded. 'I'd be interested to see how I go at a higher altitude,' he said, before adding confidently, 'I reckon I'd be okay.'

I grinned. 'Yeah, you've probably got the bloody physiology for hard climbing at altitude,' I said. 'It wouldn't surprise me.'

'I guess, wherever I climb, I'd like to be at the forefront of technical mountaineering,' Jamie continued. 'I want to be constantly pushing my own standards, and through that, hopefully inspire others to do the same. It shouldn't just be about yourself.'

FIVE

To describe and understand the crux of it all—*why do I climb?*—terms like 'flow', 'deep play', and 'in the zone' come to mind. For most people, these might seem obscure expressions that hold little meaning or place in their everyday lives. But, for others like myself, they capture the epitome of what's important to us.

These terms are an attempt to represent a time when we are faced with a great challenge, usually with severe consequences if we fail. We believe we have the skills to meet that challenge and, in doing so, may become totally immersed in the immediacy of any given moment. Perhaps we reach a focussed, and what some like to describe as a meditative, state. Time and difficulty pass without notice. Despite the risk, we are completely attuned to surmounting whatever is before us. Any thought of failure, something that may have held us back, is forgotten.

Plenty has been written about such mental states. Non-climbers use definitions of them to try to understand why climbers and other extreme risk-takers—the so-called 'adrenaline junkies'—do what they do. These states could just as easily be labelled as leading to a type of delinquency. On the other hand, climbers and other extreme adventurers might refer to the terms as a means of self-justification. They are the 'Holy Grail' of an experience or of an accumulation of experiences.

Author Maria Coffey explored the consequences of climbers and their risk taking in her thought-provoking book, *Where the Mountain Casts Its Shadow*. Through a series of interviews and anecdotes, she drew attention to the feelings of those bereaved by climbing accidents. Essentially, Coffey addressed two questions: what motivates people to climb, and what is the cost of climbing to family and friends?

Describing climbing as the 'dazzling brilliance of risk and the darkness of its shadows', Coffey asked why anyone would choose to love a person who repeatedly risks his or her life in the mountains. And, often, the climbers she interviewed were unable to explain why they couldn't withdraw from their high-risk addiction, even after losing close mountaineering friends to it.

I understand Coffey's findings only too well. Over the years, I have tried to ascertain my own reasons for climbing, something that would also make sense of becoming lost in the moment. I like to refer to it as reaching a 'sublime' state, a word that can be defined as 'causing deep emotions and feelings of wonder or joy'.

Historically, the word sublime was specifically linked to fear. In 1757, Irishman Edmund Burke published a short essay with a rather long title: *A Philosophical Enquiry into the Origin of Our Ideas of the Sublime and Beautiful.* Burke wanted to account for passions evoked in the human mind by what he called 'terrible objects' (for example, standing on the edge of a cliff or before a raging sea).

Any wild landscapes that induced feelings of intimidation, or even fear, Burke termed as 'subliminal sights'. Perhaps it was because he deemed the landscapes too big or chaotic to comprehend. Whereas beauty might have a relaxing effect, the sublime 'is productive of the strongest emotion which the mind is capable of feeling'. Burke claimed that experiencing the sublime meant drawing close, but not too close, to those 'terrible objects'. If beauty was proportioned and measured, then the sublime was tumultuous and unpredictable.

For me, reaching a sublime state during climbing is about being *so* in the moment that every other concern or thought loses consideration. Sometimes this has occurred while I have had a climbing partner. Other times I have been in the mountains alone. Usually, the more committing the climb, the greater my sense of disconnect.

Climbing unroped with another friend, Kynan Bazley, on the north buttress of Mount Hopkins, I discovered that the exposure of falling was something I could almost embrace. Despite not knowing how difficult the climbing above would be, or even if the line we had chosen *was* climbable, I continued to move up without fear of the consequences should I slip.

On Mount Hopkins, and during other climbs, I've found that these states of mind tend not to last very long. Indeed, I believe it is their fleeting nature that makes them so alluring. Our constant craving drives us. The law of diminishing returns doesn't seem to apply.

Along with the prospect of experiencing fleeting moments

of internal peace, I also need to embrace, or at least accept, the essence of uncertainty. The unknown. The changing elements. For without uncertainty, there can be no challenge. Deciding to commit to a climb, or even a specific move, is something I try to leave for the last moment. I prefer having as much information as possible. This way, I can better recognise and understand the risks involved and then what I must do to avoid or mitigate them.

When I first see a mountain, from a distance, I usually find that it exhibits a certain tranquillity. Upon moving closer, its mood changes—or at least that's how it feels to me. Standing at the base of a climb is when I doubt myself the most. It is in that moment, as close as I can get before starting my ascent, that I lose all perspective of what lies ahead. The view of the climb becomes distorted, an even weightier proposal. I am dwarfed by the sheer size of the mountain, as well as by all of my insecurities.

To cope, I have trained myself to focus on small things: retying my boot laces; adjusting my harness; unfurling the rope again; taking another sip of water; engaging in small talk with my climbing partner; feeling the reassuring weight of my ice axes. Then, finally, I commit to taking that first measured movement upwards.

There have been times when I have hated myself for this perceived weakness, for my hesitancy. But, with the passing years and decades, I have also come to accept it. There are plenty of situations I can recall when this added caution has kept me, and others around me, safer. And then, once I am engaged in the climb, my inhibitions tend to fall away.

The air is dry. Cold. It grasps my lungs during each breath. My insides are warmed from the steepness of the ascent, but my fingers and toes remain numb. There is the sound of my breathing, laboured, but steady. My boots clomp over broken rock. The karabiners and ice screws clipped to my harness jangle. There may be a few words of care between friends, and perhaps the raucous yet eerie cry from a kea flying overhead. (How long will these endangered mountain parrots remain our alpine companions, before slipping into extinction?)

I am here to enquire. To make sense of contours on the map. To fill a blank in the guidebook. Likely I have been awake for hours, having risen from an uncomfortable night well before the dawn to ferret away with various bits of a climbing kit and to find a way in the dark. With first light comes a revelation that, unsurprisingly, I still have a long way to go if I hope to reach the summit, and then get down safely.

Time passes as I gain height. I will have to pause again in a while, regain my breath, and look up. Study what surrounds me, reevaluate everything—the terrain, the weather, the wellness of my climbing partner, the sometimes-fragile nature of my own motivation to continue. The unseen summit feels as far away as ever. As any challenge of this magnitude should.

I am nervous about what might lie ahead but also excited by the prospect. Thoughts crowd my mind, mostly questions that I need to consider an answer for: *Has the wind changed direction? Is that wispy cloud over the next mountain the beginning of another storm? How long do we have? How fatigued am I? How badly do I want to reach the top? Is it worth the effort?*

Experiencing the environment in this way invigorates me. I am tired but energised. My desire encourages focus and the commitment needed to succeed.

Considering all of this, it probably comes as no surprise that certain aspects to the mountain, to any mountain that I connect with, become humanised. Personalised. Climbing a mountain is personal to me. It matters. For a time, nothing else exists in my thoughts. Nothing else can exist. I am consumed by what I crave, and by what I don't know.

If only this is where it ends.

'How could we have foreseen that such a magnificent day would end in death?' wrote Aat Vervoorn—one of my favourite mountaineering authors—in his book *Beyond the Snowline*. 'A blue day under the crystalline sun of midwinter, on which the mountains were carved precisely by the frost out of light and shadow and the air did not become mild until midday. The ice of Mount Sefton soared above us, leaping forward through the transparent atmosphere as the car rounded the last bend in the road: pure whiteness, the upper slopes blazing light, momentarily framed between the black cliffs of Sebastopol and the bulk of Mount Wakefield.'

Later, while searching for a fellow climber who was overdue returning after a day in the mountains, Aat came across a body at the base of a climb: 'It was Bruce. He was lying on his back down the slope, his left arm curved as if to guard his head against a fall, right arm outstretched, its fist clenched in pain. He had been wearing his orange singlet to catch some afternoon sun. On the rocks above, just out from the cliff, lay his watch, its glass broken; it had stopped at twenty to three.'

Aat was writing about the death of one of his best friends, talented mountaineer and fellow guide Bruce Jenkinson. Bruce had gone out to solo a climb, and had never made it back.

Climb in the mountains for long enough and chances are

you will lose a friend, a partner, a loved one. The inevitability of it is something I as a climber must accept, but then be able to push from my mind, especially while I am in the mountains. When the worst outcome occurs, all anyone can do is try to cope with the aftermath. There is the grief of loss, but also the eventual re-justification of choosing to do something that carries such personal cost, and that can affect so many other people afterwards. When you get right down to it, there is no rational way to justify the obvious selfishness of my actions.

Years before I met Jamie, I used to climb with another good friend, Guy White. In 1999, Guy invited me to meet him in the Bregaglia Mountain Range in the north of Italy, on its border with Switzerland. We climbed as many of the classic granite spires and faces in the Val di Mello as we could manage. That time spent with Guy, and those routes we attempted, remain among the purest and most enjoyable climbing experiences of my life.

A few weeks later, Guy took a short slip on a climb while waiting for others to join him at a belay ledge. The fall wasn't far, but it was far enough to take his life. I wasn't with my friend at the time of his accident, having left to return to New Zealand, and part of me felt guilty because of that. It was like I had abandoned him. *If I had been there to climb with Guy, perhaps he would still be alive.* Of course, that was unlikely. But, the thought stayed with me, nagging at my psyche for months afterwards.

It took a long time to rediscover my love for mountaineering after Guy died. Undoubtedly it affected my decision-making on future climbs and, I believe, contributed to my increasingly conservative attitude in terms of risk and safety. I learned a new way to measure the likelihood and consequence of my actions, while also assessing the mood of the mountain and my motivation to climb it.

Now, climbing with Jamie, Kynan, Mat, my wife Shelley, or any other partner is when I feel this concern most acutely. I feel responsible for their safety. My moves and choices affect them. As a climbing team, there is an unspoken contract between us that should be adhered to at all times. We are joined, and not just by thin strands of a rope. We must return home together to remain whole in ourselves.

SIX

Jamie's axes dinked at hard, blue ice. The front points on his crampons also scraped for purchase, scratching like fingernails across a blackboard, and his torso remained poised above the depths of a seemingly bottomless crevasse. An eerie-sounding wind whooshed over the summits high above us. Somewhere much closer, water dripped like a ticking clock.

'Watch me!' Jamie called.

'All good, mate,' I shouted back. 'You're looking solid.' The rope tied between us slithered over the narrow ramp of glacier beneath my boots. Jamie hadn't placed an ice screw yet. If he slipped, he'd pendulum tens of metres right into the crevasse.

My wife, Shelley, another friend, Kester Brown, and I watched Jamie's progress with keen interest. This was the only way forward. Despite the tenseness of the situation, I still felt a sudden urge to peer down into the blue-black of the deep cleft.

Now Jamie was talking to himself, his muttered words lost

across the chasm. *Should I offer him more encouragement?* When I was much younger—a novice climber—I realised one day that the more animated my belayer was in complimenting me, the direr the situation actually seemed from their perspective.

I tried again: 'Just take your time, Jamie. No rush, mate.'

But this statement wasn't right either. Early morning sunlight had already arched over the remote Stevenson Glacier that we were trying to navigate. Forty kilometres further west, a dark, thickening cloud had been oozing in from the edge of the Tasman Sea. The next front wasn't far off. The day was getting away from us, and we hadn't even reached the start of our proposed route.

I doubted Jamie was paying attention to anything other than the ice and how little his front points were penetrating it. He was partly deaf, so he probably couldn't even hear what I was saying. I was calling out reassurances to make myself feel better.

It was still early in the summer alpine season, yet already cavernous gaps had opened in the glaciers around us. I remained hopeful everything would work out. My friend could bend the reality of climbing sequences, making them appear easier than they were. Despite the difficulties, I was sure he'd deal with this.

Jamie reset his axes, and the tinkering sound of falling ice echoed across the morning air.

Kester quietly munched on a muesli bar as he watched.

'That's a bomb site over there,' he said. 'I think Jamie will be coming back.'

'You reckon?' I replied. 'Christ, how are we going to get through this bloody maze?'

Kester offered no solutions. Not inclined to get worked

up about anything other than burnt coffee, he turned to look across this rugged pocket of our Southern Alps with a wistful gaze. To the north, the Stevenson and other feeder glaciers plunged over weathered rock slabs on the western flanks of Mount Elie de Beaumont and Mount Walter. To the south, the ice fields were warped back from the more shattered, blocky rifts that held up Mount Green.

We were hoping to tackle the unclimbed west rib of Walter, a chipped arch of coarse greywacke half a kilometre high. However, even reaching it was proving difficult. I kicked the ice with my crampons, before finding my eyes drawn again to the darkness of the nearby crevasse.

Two hundred metres below us, the Stevenson fingered into the broad palm of the larger Spencer Glacier; it, in turn, sagged between the barren knuckles of the Drummond Ridge and the Burton Ridge, before disintegrating into the Callery River hundreds more metres down the valley. Even from this distance, the unbraided river appeared turbulent and restless. Aoraki / Mount Cook was a few kilometres farther southwest, hidden behind serrated summits of the Main Divide.

There hadn't been a first ascent recorded in this part of Westland Tai Poutini National Park since 1984. As far as I knew, no one had even attempted a route from the Stevenson in the past decade. Looking at the terrain we still had to negotiate, it was easy to understand why not.

At last, Jamie reached the other side of the crevasse and clambered over a low fold of ice. He disappeared from view. Shelley was perched on a divot in the glacier a few metres behind Kester and me. She inched forward to try to glimpse what Jamie might be seeing. Moments later, curses floated over the void, and Jamie returned into view. He shook his head. Kester shrugged his shoulders, probably already thinking about heading back to our tents to brew another round of fresh coffee.

My wife smiled at me, and then started cramping back across the slope we had traversed at first light. She skirted a short ice cliff and vanished down a snowy ramp in a different direction from where we were camped. I figured she must have been searching for another way through the jumble of crevasses. Shelley has a stubborn streak to her.

Jamie's earlier encouragement at the dinner party to find somewhere new to climb had remained stuck in my mind. So, I went searching. I perused maps, old guidebooks, and alpine journals, comparing them with my own previous experiences to come up with a suitable objective. I noted that first ascents in the Spencer Glacier area of the Southern Alps tapered off in the early 1980s. Yet the few people that climbed in the area then wrote about 'good quality rock', at least by Kiwi alpine standards.

The Spencer Glacier area had been in the back of my mind for some time. I'd first spied the auburn hues of the west rib of Walter back in 2000 while guiding on the Franz Josef Glacier. Every clear morning for the next two years, I carried coffee outside of the small cottage I'd rented in the nearby coastal settlement of Ōkārito, to see the mountains. I leaned against the railing, swatted sandflies, and faced the sunrise. The silhouettes of Elie de Beaumont, Walter, and Green craned over thick, dark rainforests and the white splodge of the Spencer and other glaciers.

Day after day, I stared at that same view. Sometimes

a warbled morning sun made the mountains shimmer in the sky. Other times, in flat, sepia-toned light, the summits seemed close enough to touch. I promised myself that I would, someday, try to climb them. Yet after a number of forays from the Franz, I came to realise the difficulties involved. In the summer, glacial thaw cut off the western access. With no icy bridges to clamber down, all that remained were steep, impassable walls of rocky detritus—crumbling greywacke at its worst.

The most logical approach seemed to be from the east, traversing this country's longest glacier, the Tasman, and then climbing over the Main Divide. Despite being a generally straightforward hike of around twenty-five kilometres, it took more than a decade for me to carry out that plan.

Shelley reappeared on the snow slope below us. She was breathing heavily from the exertion, but grinning. 'There might be a way over here,' she called out, pointing northwards with her axe. 'We can't get down the glacier, but I think we can get off the ice and onto the ridge.'

The rest of us shuffled over to where my wife had indicated. There was a wide gap between glacier and rock, but a narrow, fragile-looking tongue of ice jutted out over a constantly rumbling ice cliff. Access across the tongue looked tenuous; it might just go.

Ice collapsed nearby with a loud *whompf*, making us all twitch. The glacier gave a gentle shudder and settled again. I quickly established an anchor—and myself—in a nearby crevasse; that way, I wouldn't have to be the first to test the ice tongue. When no one else made any moves toward the edge, Kester sighed. Since he was the tallest, it seemed appropriate that he should try before the rest of us.

Kester gave his ice axe a good thunk into the undercut slip in the glacier. He peered over. 'Don't like this much,' he mumbled.

My friend shuffled his crampons for a few seconds before finally re-hooking his axe on a last, thin, icy protuberance. Extending his long legs, Kester reached for the rock. He snared a narrow ledge with his crampon, let out a small 'woo-hoo', and scrambled up the broken ground to set a belay.

Shelley, easily the most vertically challenged in our group, had to swing one leg repeatedly, building up momentum before she could stab across the gap. Her crampons scraped against the rock as she searched for purchase. Once stable, she leaned out, draped her axe over a rock flake on the other side, and then lunged the rest of her body over.

Jamie climbed down the edge, peered over, said, 'Bugger that,' and clipped his axe to his harness.

'Give me some slack,' he called up to me. Then he launched himself across the void, flying like a movie character. Somehow, he managed to stick to the small ledge on the other side.

'Sometimes I just do stuff without thinking about it too much,' he said in a nonchalant tone as if the excuse he was making could somehow be considered valid.

When it was my turn, the others shouted, 'Go for it.' But the prospect of repeating Jamie's aerial feat made my ageing knees quiver. I sunk the pick of my axe as deep as it would go into the ice, clasped it with two hands, and pushed one leg out behind me until it clattered against the rock. Once stemmed between glacier and rock, and upon realising that I could bridge the void, I breathed a sigh of relief.

At the belay, I paused to take in this narrow buttress of red greywacke that we were about to climb. The rock curved towards the skyline in a graceful arch, a totem that enticed us upwards for hundreds of metres. I couldn't help laughing. We'd made it across to the rib of unclimbed rock, a place of uncertainty, the kind of place that climbers, perhaps, treasure most.

Kester and Shelley were already heading off on the next pitch, a steep slab with desk-sized missing chunks. I suggested to Jamie that we follow a short bulge to the left to stay out from underneath them in case of falling rocks. Jamie handed me the rack. The weight felt reassuring in my grasp.

The call of a kea—sounding like an elongated cry of the vowels in its own name—echoed from somewhere above. I looked up. Red-and-green wings flashed across the air. A foot tall, with a powerful beak and claws, these native mountain parrots are known for getting into mischief. Their antics include hopping into tent vestibules, hacking up smelly, seed-riddled bile like a dinner offering, and hopping out again; worrying a pack strap until the pack falls apart; and tearing a tent to shreds in a shark-like frenzy. I hoped that if the kea spotted our tents, it would choose Jamie's over mine.

The coarseness of the rock rasped against my fingers—a reassuring feeling, like a distant memory of past experiences. The patina of the sandstone in front of me was almost sunset red. Fingertip cracks split its near-vertical surface, and a thin ramp angled like a tree branch across the bulge, up and left. I slinked along the ramp, ferreting at dead-end cracks. Once I'd finally found a notch deep enough, I slipped a cam into it and, slightly higher, a nut. I clipped the rope through them and relaxed my grip on the holds. Now I had the confidence to tiptoe up for another few metres.

But then the edges and the cracks began to vanish. The air was still. Another kea called in the distance. *This is when everything fades and sharpens. This is the time that matters. Breathe. Keep breathing.* I slipped one hand after another into my chalk bag, more a meditative preparation than anything else, and continued the traverse. A vague ledge up and farther left looked like my next respite. Smooth, precise moves slipped by. I felt as if I was immersed within the intricate texture of the rock.

Time passed without notice. Then a muffled shout rose from Jamie, indicating that I was near the end of the rope. I scanned for somewhere to belay. This awkward corner I was bridging would have to do. Two small nuts dropped key-like into a thin crack, and I shouted back down in the direction of the rope. Shifting weight from one leg to the other, I looked up, trying to judge how much farther we had to go. A mossy rooflet hid the terrain above. The climb gave nothing away.

Hours later, the summit ridge came almost as a shock. I staggered for a moment, trying to readjust to the sudden change in geography, from the steepness of the wall to a nearly flat rock shelf. Broad ledges created a bench along the eastern side of the Main Divide in both directions. A few metres behind me, the glacier that wound back to our tents seemed to float in the evening light.

The sun's warmth filled me with renewed energy. As Jamie seconded the last few metres, a crimson glow drew across the mountaintops and tinged the glaciers pink. The rest of my party reached the top soon after. Jamie wasn't into hugs, but I grabbed him anyway. Kester shied away, muttering something about being all sweaty. Red glimmers caught in the tiny wisps of hair sticking out from under Shelley's helmet. We also hugged, not needing to say anything to each other.

At its best, climbing is absolute fun; there is joy in reaching a summit or a high point. Achieving that goal, I felt light, almost like I could lift from the earth if I wanted to. Memories of climbing trees with my brothers were rekindled, a similar act repeated with my wife and good friends. There was more complexity here, especially in terms of equipment and terrain, but the essence felt the same. I embraced the success, but more so the feeling of being above it all for a time. Of being free.

The where, the what, and the why of climbing had been answered emphatically. There was no doubt in my mind. Looking across the other mountains and glaciers and valleys spread beneath our feet felt like flying, drifting on a soft breeze high above the land, with the ability to view everything and the opportunity to go anywhere. What was below could remain there, forgotten until I wished to return.

The others started cramponing down the gentle snow slope, but I took a few extra minutes to look back over the Spencer. Through the low clouds that choked most of the valley, I tried to eke out other crannies worth investigating. A long rippling slab ran up the western flank of Elie de Beaumont. *Can we reach it?* I couldn't see whether the narrow glacier beside it went all the way to the névé below, or if it too cracked apart and disintegrated against the mountainside.

The last of the evening light merged the high peaks around me with the off-white cloud and the snow, the distant blue of the sky and the ocean. The view softened and became hazy, fading slowly toward the night until everything felt like one thing.

Now, thinking again about this adventure with my wife and good mates, there's one other moment from it that sticks in my mind. It was mid-afternoon after another climb, and we had already returned to our campsite near the saddle between Mount Green and Mount Walter. The sun was on its way to meeting the Tasman Sea. The warmth of the day and all of the previous days' exercise meant that three of us were happy just to laze in our tents.

Jamie seemed restless. He alternated between pacing around in the snow and staring off towards the mountains that surrounded us.

'I might go for a wander,' he said after a while.

'Oh, yeah?' I replied.

'Back down to that rock we saw. Just for a look, eh? I shouldn't be too long.'

'Okay. Have fun.'

Both Kester and I noticed that Jamie had quietly slipped his climbing shoes into his pack, along with a jacket and water bottle, before fixing his crampons to his boots and then heading off to the top of the icefall we had been using for access to the rock walls west of the Main Divide.

'What do you reckon?' I asked Kester.

'Hard to say,' my friend replied. 'He could.'

Kester, Shelley, and I all figured what Jamie might be up to. We had previously spotted a steep shield of compact rock close to one of the new routes we'd completed. It looked climbable—*just*—but didn't have any cracks for protection. Higher up, it joined onto one of our routes, where the angle of the rock lessened and the climbing would become easier again.

At the time, Jamie had commented how good the climbing looked on it. But, like the rest of us, he'd recognised that it couldn't be climbed with a rope as there weren't any places to belay at the end of each pitch. The three of us reckoned that Jamie was heading back down to look at soloing it.

Arguably, soloing is the purest form of climbing. There is no encumbrance of ropes and placing protection, and no climbing partner to worry about. There is just movement. Of course, above a certain height, falling is not an option.

When climbing moderate terrain, most mountaineers would choose to solo because using a rope takes too long and the chance of slipping is minimal. But, on a climb like what Jamie was possibly considering—especially something that hadn't been done before—there was no way of telling how hard it could be.

At first, I wondered whether he would commit to the route. I also wondered why he hadn't mentioned his intent to us beforehand. Then I figured he didn't want to have to deal with my likely criticism of unsafe climbing choices. He wanted to be able to make his decision alone. I lay in the tent and waited—perhaps *hoped* is a more accurate term—for my friend to return.

An hour or so later, I heard footsteps in the snow. I poked my head out. Jamie was coming back from the saddle rather than the top of Mount Walter.

'So, you didn't climb it then,' I said with a smile.

Jamie glanced at me, and then he looked away for a few moments before saying anything. 'Was it that obvious?'

'Oh, yeah.'

Jamie set down on his pack. 'I really wanted to,' he said. 'Even put my shoes on and played on the first bit to see how the rock felt. I looked up at what was above. Totally reckon I could have done it, too.'

'Probably, mate,' I replied. 'What stopped you?'

'I don't know. I guess it's where doing something like that can lead you. There's no end, is there? You keep trying harder and harder solos until you get committed on something you can't do. It's bloody tempting. But, once I start...'

'Well, for what it's worth, I reckon you made the right call.'

'Yeah,' Jamie said, not looking entirely convinced. 'I think I did, too.'

SEVEN

What constitutes a great climb? An aesthetic line. Stable weather. Motivated companions who are also competent mountaineers. Solid rock and firm ice. The right amount of challenge. And an unknown outcome.

These ingredients create the opportunity for adventure. I don't always need to reach the top of a mountain to consider a particular route a great climb. Other times, the summit is necessary; it holds more significance.

Returning to Christchurch after such a rewarding trip with Jamie, Shelley, and Kester, I couldn't wait for the next opportunity. I was back at work, but my mind remained up in the cliffs and snowfields. Days dragged by. I couldn't concentrate. My focus was on *climbing*.

Climbing partnerships are often an integral part of successful mountaineering, and our recent trip to Mount Walter was indicative of that. We each had our strengths and combined these well as a team. All four of us stepped up during different parts of the trip, either in terms of route finding or leading difficult cruxes. Our individual skills and knowledge made us stronger as an overall unit.

I have had a few different climbing partners over the years. Before I met Jamie, I spent many seasons climbing with another friend, Mat Woods. Mat was studying at Otago University while I was managing Bivouac Outdoor in Dunedin, and we headed into the mountains nearly every free weekend. We had some close calls, but we were also there for each other. Whoever felt the need to lead a climb or a particular pitch did so. If neither wanted to climb, we would happily turn around and go home.

Together, Mat and I explored as many corners of the Hopkins and surrounding valleys as we could find. If the forecast was poor, we would either ascend to the base of a climb we wanted to do, researching the approach to see if any good bivouac sites existed nearby, or we would climb the easier descent. All the time we were increasing our knowledge of the land, improving our chances of success. The more we climbed together, the more confident we grew in our skills and teamwork. And, regardless of how knackered we were after a climb, we'd usually had so much fun together that we couldn't wait for the next weekend to go again. My time at work during the week was the period to rest and recover.

As our team dynamic developed, it allowed us to tackle more challenging objectives. We believed in each other, and that helped us also believe more in our own abilities. Climbing with Mat set the bar for every partnership that followed. If any prospective partner was more interested in getting something climbed rather than looking out for the other's welfare, then they were never a partner for long. It was, and still is, more important to me *who* I climb with rather than *what* I climb.

Climbing partnerships can take many forms. Experience levels may not be the same but they can still have worth. Finding a partner who is stronger adds security as you develop your own skills.

The first five years, the apprenticeship in a climber's life, are said to be the most risky. We don't know what we don't know. There is a blindness, or at least a naivety, to our desire. During my early years, my keenness clouded the realisation that I understood so little about what held mountains together and when parts of them were more likely to fall apart. And odther than small moments of being scared, I hadn't yet discovered what my limits were, both physical and mental.

I was lucky enough to find someone with greater knowledge to help guide me through my first seasons in the mountains. I met another climber with much more experience, and who had served their own apprenticeship and was willing to share what they had learned.

The last time I had lived in Christchurch—before moving with Shelley—was during the early to mid-1990s. Jamie would still have been in primary school while I was pretending to study at Lincoln University and, more importantly, discovering rock climbing and then mountaineering with some of the other students. One classmate, Glenn Familton, boarded with a mountain guide. That was the first time I met Marty Schmidt—someone who would go on to be one of my main climbing mentors.

Marty had recently moved to the city with his family, having chosen it as a base for his professional guiding business. Glenn described Marty as a 'hard taskmaster at home', with new projects around the house always in need of completion. Glenn reckoned he came to study at university to get away from all the chores that Marty found, and so he could rest.

I remember Marty often having to look after his two children whenever we went rock climbing together. Denali, his son, was already old enough to safely clamber around the bottom of a crag on his own. But Marty would need to tie knots in the end of the rope around the younger Sequoia, hoping that he could complete a route before she managed to undo them and crawl away towards whatever mischief she could find.

One day, Marty offered to take Glenn and me on one of his expeditions overseas, but Glenn reckoned Marty would load our packs too much, expecting us to carry the same as the legendary Sherpa of Nepal. But I didn't feel that way. The tales Marty told of climbing the world's highest mountains reminded me of the great expedition books I had read as a youngster. I would loved to have gone. At the time, it seemed that his life was one long, epic adventure.

It was a nice surprise to find that, after a period overseas, Marty had also recently returned to Christchurch around the same time that Shelley and I moved north from Dunedin.

In my mind, Marty had always been a bit of an enigma. While much of the New Zealand climbing community probably hadn't heard of him, he was one of this country's most successful high-altitude climbers. As far as I knew, he was the only Kiwi consistently climbing 8000-metre peaks without using supplementary oxygen.

American-born, Marty had lived in New Zealand on and off since 1988. With a German mother and Polish father, who'd both immigrated to the United States, Marty had grown up in California. In his early years, through the 1970s and 80s, he'd spent summers either hiking in the Sierra Mountains or climbing in Yosemite Valley with the likes of Ron Kauk, Dale Bard, Jim Bridwell, and John Bachar. Marty had been rubbing shoulders and sharing leads with some of America's most revered climbers.

'Climbing was ground-up in those days,' Marty explained to me one morning when we caught up for coffee at his home. 'There was no coming down from the top to inspect the route. Everything was an adventure back then.'

Marty explained that his biggest influence at the time was British climber Ed Hart. 'I was fifteen when we hooked up,' he explained. 'Ed dragged me up a number of the Valley test pieces. Those were special experiences. They helped instill in me my whole philosophy around climbing, and later around guiding.'

After the Sierras and Yosemite, Marty progressed to climbing expeditions in Alaska and South America, before finally deciding to settle in New Zealand. When he first moved here, Marty quickly considered it his home. 'Everyone has a calling inside,' he said. 'For me, it was to live here in this beautiful land.'

While based in New Zealand, Marty developed his mountain guiding career, which slowly but surely grew a loyal client base. Eventually, Marty's guiding progressed into the higher mountains.

'I guess my first personal high-altitude experience was on Denali,' he said. 'I was working as a para-rescue man with the United States Air Force at the time, and got it into my head to climb Denali to help with my skillset for rescue.'

The year was 1983, two years before I would leave high school. Marty successfully climbed Denali three times that season, including the challenging Cassin Ridge and a first ascent of the West Buttress Direct. While climbing on Mount

Denali, Marty often saw other guides attending to large numbers of clients.

'That style of guiding just doesn't appeal to me,' he said. 'I'm not criticising it, but I'd see three guides and nine clients on Denali, all bunched together. Even at a three-to-one ratio, I'd find it hard to be fully attuned to each individual. For me, climbing with a client is about developing a relationship and exploring the full gambit of the mountaineering experience as a small team.'

In the big-money game of high-altitude guiding, the largest commercial companies chase increasing numbers of clients. Ropes are fixed and piles of oxygen cylinders cached by high-altitude Sherpa. Marty had a different approach. Rather than reducing the mountain to the standard of the client, he tried to raise the client's skills to match the mountain.

'It's a philosophy that's been around since the days of Zurbriggen and Fitzgerald,' he said. 'Zurbriggen was the guide, but they worked together through whatever the mountain threw at them. They made the first ascent of Aconcagua in that style, and almost of Mount Cook as well.'

2010 was an especially significant year for Marty. In May, he set out to climb a new route on one of the world's highest mountains—Makalu (8463m)—with a friend and fellow guide, American Chris Warner.

'We picked a line on the south face, then got through the lower glacier and ABC [Advanced Base Camp] up to Camp One,' Marty recalled. 'It had been a dry season, so there wasn't much snow around. When we got hit by rockfall, Chris and I decided it wasn't safe enough to continue.'

The pair angled over to the nearby southeast ridge, ahead of a British team. 'We helped fix seven hundred metres of line for them before Chris came down with a suspected pulmonary embolism,' Marty explained. 'It wasn't worth the risk even staying at that altitude to see if his condition improved. I needed to get him off the mountain as quickly as I could.'

It took nine hours to descend the fixed lines through steep terrain, and the next day, Marty got Chris safely out in a helicopter. Chris would end up making a full recovery. But, for the time being, Marty was left on the mountain alone.

'It was then that I came up with the idea of trying to solo Makalu,' Marty reflected. 'I filled a pack from Base Camp and walked around to the north side. Above ABC, I ended up linking up with another guy, and we soloed up into position to try for the summit. The weather wasn't settled and he decided to turn back, but I had enough food to stay, so I set up camp at 7700 metres.'

Meanwhile, another large team from Ukraine had been attempting a difficult new line on Makalu, between the West Pillar and the Yugoslav Route. A team of twelve climbers took turns forging over sixty new pitches. On May 23, the day before Marty decided to leave his campsite and head up, three of the Ukrainian team went for the summit. They topped out and, in poor visibility, tried to descend the north side of the mountain.

'At 1:00 a.m. on the 24th, I left my camp,' Marty told me. 'The weather wasn't that settled, but I was feeling good and decided to push for the summit.'

About an hour later, Marty came across another climber who appeared to be lost. 'I managed to get him back to my tracks and then help him down to my camp,' Marty said. 'He told me there was someone else further up the mountain. I turned around, headed back up, and found the second guy after another hour and a half.' The second climber had lost his gloves, and was suffering from dehydration. 'I got him back down to my camp as well, then brewed up some water to try and re-energise both of them with,' Marty explained. 'Then they told me there was still one more.'

Marty found the third climber at around 8200 metres. He was slumped over on his pack. 'That's what happens at 8000 metres if you sit down when you're exhausted,' Marty said. 'You just don't get up again. So, I slapped him to try and rouse him, got some Dex into him, and started dragging him back down.' (Dex is shorthand for dexamethasone, a high-altitude medication commonly used by climbers.)

After being hauled about two hundred metres by Marty, the third climber recovered enough to try and get to his feet. 'Another hundred metres and he was doing better,' Marty said. 'By the time I got him back to my tent, I knew he would be okay.'

By this time, the first two Ukrainian climbers had recovered enough to descend unassisted. Marty settled the third into his tent.

'When I judged he was fine, I decided I still wanted to try for the summit,' Marty said. 'So, despite the weather not being the best, I turned around and headed back up.'

After summiting, Marty returned to his high camp. Soloing Makalu was a huge enough achievement, but Marty had managed it *after* putting his own life at risk to help other climbers. The following day, he continued helping the Ukrainians down to Advanced Base Camp.

Marty's attitude toward helping others in need also extended to his approach to guiding clients. 'I'm not interested in just getting a whole lot of people to a summit and back down, then saying "see you later,"' he explained to me. 'I want to test them. I want to take them to their limit, just like the older climbers like Ed Hart did for me back in

Yosemite. It's how we grow as climbers, how we understand more about ourselves and about the environment around us.'

I realised that Marty was more than apt at this. When we first went rock climbing together again, he asked me: 'So, Paul, what are you weakest at on rock right now?'

'Cracks, I guess.'

'Well, we should go and climb some cracks, then.'

Next thing I knew, he was asking what training I did for climbing, which hills I ran up, how long each run took, what type of food I ate, even when I went to the toilet. I could see him storing all of this information away, processing it so he understood better what would make me tick in the mountains. This was the sign of a particularly attentive guide, and person.

'With my clients,' Marty explained, 'I might go and visit them months before we are due to climb. We'll train together, eat together, live together. That way we'll have the time to build a relationship that is essential, I think, for a successful climb. And that's especially important when you start going for the eight thousand-ers.'

Marty's philosophy for his clients on the highest peaks in the world was no Sherpa assistance (above Base Camp), no bottled oxygen and no drugs. 'I'm flexible with it,' he said. 'On a summit day, I might suggest my client uses extra O2, especially as a safety buffer. But it's a style I like to stick to if I can. If we don't summit, for whatever reason, we evaluate, maybe go away and train some more or build up with other peaks before coming back. I like to work and grow with my clients.'

This approach saw a number of Marty's clients sticking with him for twenty years or more, an ongoing relationship that most high-altitude guides would be jealous of. I also understood how much effort Marty put into building the team dynamic between his clients and himself. This resonated strongly with my own beliefs around the importance of good teamwork.

It was great to spend time with Marty again after so many years being out of touch. We caught up for coffee as often as possible. During one catch-up, Marty asked me about my own mountaineering aspirations. I mentioned my recent climbing trips overseas to the Greater Ranges, how much I had enjoyed the expeditions but also how I had sometimes struggled to acclimatise to the higher mountains.

Marty was convinced I could train my body to perform better at altitude. He then offered to take Shelley and me on one of his expeditions, to help us achieve some of our goals in the mountains overseas. I half-agreed without thinking too much about what climbing with Marty on a big mountain might entail.

Straight away, he began to put a plan in place. When he suggested we should go for a practice run together, I tried for a lame excuse before suggesting that perhaps Shelley may be a better option. I wasn't sure whether it was because of his wiry build, or that mischievous glint in his eye, but I became decidedly nervous about him forcing every last sap of energy out of me during the training, not to mention the physical and mental discomfort that would undoubtedly go with it.

I then asked Marty about the importance of having a physiology that naturally coped with altitude. Marty agreed that some people are better suited to climbing at altitude, but then he went on to convince me that we all had the ability to climb high; we just had to work out how to increase our own limits as safely as possible.

'I believe you can climb higher mountains if you choose to, Paul,' he said. 'It's just about unlocking the potential in your body, and then working out what is the best way to achieve that.'

In an effort to change the subject from my inadequacies at altitude, I asked Marty about his own goals. Marty said he had some bold climbs coming up, both in New Zealand and overseas. I knew he had recently completed a new route on the challenging south face of Aoraki / Mount Cook with an up-and-coming mountain guide, Elke Braun-Elwert. I hadn't met Elke, but Marty talked enthusiastically about her endurance and ability in the mountains.

Generally, Marty wasn't one to go on much about his own projects until after they had been completed. Instead, he chose to focus on encouraging others to get out there and try things for themselves.

'Despite the relatively low altitude, New Zealand is a great place to climb,' he said. 'All the ingredients are here for someone to be able to improve all of their climbing skills, and then to take them to the Greater Ranges if they want to.'

For Marty, there were three key things every climber should focus on: believe in what you do; be open to different styles; and trust in your climbing partnership. I nodded, again recognising the similarity of his approach to my own philosophy around mountaineering, one that revolved around safety and good teamwork.

Then my friend added one final piece of advice: 'If you know who you are at any given moment, you're more likely to be able to cope with whatever situation is thrown at you, either in the climbing world or in your everyday life.'

EIGHT

Our home in Christchurch was built on a finger of sand, with the Avon-Heathcote Estuary on one side and Pacific Ocean on the other. Rocking Horse Road ran the length of the narrow peninsula. Our place was a hundred metres from its southern tip, near where the waters of the Avon-Heathcote ran to the sea. There were approximately five hundred homes built between the sand dunes and mudflats, and our Southshore community seemed miles away from the urban bustle of the central city.

It was the summer of 2011. Along with writing and route setting at a local climbing gym, I had started working part-time as a sales assistant at Bivouac Outdoor. The tramping and climbing store was on Colombo Street in the middle of the city. Working there meant time away from my computer, but more importantly, provided the opportunity to buy cheap climbing gear.

Shelley, Jamie, and I kept climbing as much as we could, either at the local indoor wall, on the rock crags overlooking the city, or in the mountains whenever we could get time away that aligned with decent weather. Occasionally, I managed to catch up with Marty, but he was often overseas on another expedition.

On one Tuesday—a particular Tuesday that has become starkly etched in my mind—I was taking my lunch break from Bivouac. After eating sushi, I bought coffee from Vivace on the recently renovated Hereford Street, before taking the lift up to the sixth floor of the Vero Centre to catch up with my friend (and incredible photographer) Lee Howell. Lee and I chatted about possible projects we could work on together.

I returned to the ground floor, stepped back out onto Hereford, and headed east towards the intersection of Hereford and Colombo. The sidewalk was crowded with tourists and locals on their lunch break. Overhead, above the tall buildings, the sun was doing its best to prove the forecasters wrong. I wondered if the predicted swell would hit the coast. The improving weather might also allow for a trip into the hills in the coming weekend.

Without warning, the ground lurched violently. Chunks of masonry suddenly sheared off a shop nearby and smashed onto the footpath centimetres away from where I stood. The initial force of the earthquake knocked me from my feet. Windows shattered, and then the fronts of buildings started collapsing. The noise was deafening. People around me got hit by falling debris.

I tried to stand up, shouting at others nearby to move away from the buildings. Some did, but some chose to shelter near teetering walls. I lost sight of them as more bricks fell from above. I remember grabbing someone who was curled up on the footpath, trying to drag them into the middle of the street where they were less likely to be hit. All the time the ground roared with a deep rumbling sound. The earth was tearing itself apart.

The earthquake lasted for about twenty seconds. When it stopped, the street was filled with dust and debris. It was unrecognisable. Towards the intersection between Hereford and Colombo, a building had collapsed right across the road. The roaring sound of the earthquake had been replaced by building alarms and people screaming, shouting or crying. Some people seemed to be aimlessly running up and down the street. Some, like I, stood dazed, trying to take in what had just happened before deciding what to do next. Others lay injured on the asphalt.

Is my wife okay? I suddenly thought. Competing with thousands of residents concerned for loved ones, I tried to call and then text her, but she didn't answer either time. Through the haze, I could see people, some badly injured, trying to get out from inside the damaged buildings.

I looked towards the Vero building and thought about Lee. There, people were kicking at the broken glass doors and clambering out. I shouted to them to get away from the building and to move down towards the relative safety of the Avon's riverbanks. Some did so, but others slumped to the ground as soon as they got outside, their energy spent. At one stage, I tried to get into the Vero building foyer to look for Lee, but a line of people kept coming out.

About ten minutes after the initial quake, the first aftershock hit. Someone called out a warning. More debris fell from above, like a rockfall in the mountains. A man next to me was hit. Self-preservation kicked in and I ran.

Upon reaching the Avon, I slowed and walked south along its banks, past the Bridge of Remembrance and then down Lichfield Street towards where it intersected Colombo. Everywhere the scene was of utter chaos and destruction. Cars had been crushed by collapsed walls. People stood in small clusters and looked on in shocked disbelief. Some held pieces of clothing over wounds. A few were inert on the ground, presumably having been dragged clear. Others dug hopelessly at mounds of rubble.

I passed a man with a head wound who couldn't work out which direction the hospital was in. Since I wanted to get back to Bivouac to check on my coworkers, I managed to convince an uninjured bystander who was taking photos to help him get there.

Then my phone bleeped. It was Shelley, checking to see I was okay. Relief flooded through me that she wasn't hurt. I kept trying to text back, but couldn't get through due to an overloaded system.

How are my workmates? I rushed down the remainder of Lichfield towards Bivouac, passing a burst gas pipe that was hissing, and then a single, dazed policeman who looked like he didn't know what to deal with first.

The Bivouac building was still standing. But the glass frontage had shattered. My work colleague, Rob, stood outside, and Chris, the manager, was getting on his bicycle to go and check that his wife and children were safe. Chris and I hugged quickly and he cycled off. John, another worker and good friend, came over, covered in dust. He had just helped dig an elderly woman out from under a collapsed veranda, but didn't know if she would make it. Both directions of Colombo Street looked like a war zone.

Another policeman arrived, and he suddenly started

shouting at us: 'You have to leave! There's a gas leak.'

I wondered how to get to Shelley at her work. South along Colombo looked impassable. The only way out was east along Lichfield, and then maybe south along Manchester. I figured that at least once I was clear of the city centre, no tall buildings could fall on me.

The road was gridlocked with drivers trying to inch their way along ruptured roads while aftershocks continued and more bits of buildings fell onto the street. Stuck inside a vehicle was the last place I wanted to be with the aftershocks; I gladly went on foot instead.

I helped a Japanese couple down Lichfield, escorting the elderly woman by the arm as we weaved between the cars and stayed as far away as possible from the more fragile-looking buildings. On the corner of Lichfield and Manchester, I crouched beside a man who was lying unconscious on the ground. He was breathing and had no obvious injuries, but he was covered in dust. I held his hand. Someone arrived with a blanket, and soon after, a police car somehow managed to weave through the chaos and pull up alongside us.

Finally, I got a text through to Shelley. The best option seemed to be to walk home and meet her there.

Three hours later, after avoiding craters in the roads and watching panicked drivers motor into them at full speed, wading through sewerage and wastewater and silt, seeing slumped bridges, crushed houses, fallen trees and snapped power lines, as well as countless faces—each wide-eyed, blank, and lost—I managed to reach home.

Surprisingly, our house was still standing. But, along with most of the other dwellings along the street, it had developed a rather sharp lean. Foundations had been torn apart. The front door was blown open, deadlocks exploded outward. Flooding lapped at the concrete step, and in the backyard, small sand volcanos—*liquefaction* was a term we would later become very familiar with—erupted out of cracks in the ground. Inside, it looked like someone had let a rogue bull run riot.

After checking that all of our neighbours were okay, I scratched around in the bomb site for a gas cooker, scooped water out of the toilet cistern and made a cup of coffee. Everything that had been in the fridge was now on the floor. Power, phone, water, and sewerage were all down. I found a transistor radio and turned it on to bury the silence.

Shelley arrived home an hour later, exhausted and covered in grime. We hugged as if our lives depended on it.

At 12:51 p.m. on February 22, 2011, a cloudy summer's day with a light, offshore breeze cooling the temperature, Christchurch was blasted by a 6.3 magnitude earthquake. Nearly two hundred people were killed, mostly in two collapsing buildings, and thousands of others were injured. It was the city's second major earthquake in less than five months. In the early hours of September 4, 2010, a 7.1 magnitude shake—much deeper within the earth's crust and therefore less destructive—had thrown residents from their beds.

The city had suffered moderate damage then, but nothing compared to the damage done in the shallower and more violent February quake that followed. People lost loved ones, homes, and businesses, all in less than half a minute. For a population as small as New Zealand's, the second quake brought a city, and a country, to its knees.

But as deadly and shocking as the February earthquake was, the months following proved far more harrowing for many of Christchurch's residents. In the days after the quake, the scale and extent of the devastation became apparent; whole suburbs, businesses, roads, and lives had been destroyed. Even simple tasks, the things you take for granted like buying food, going to the toilet, or catching up with friends, became a challenge. It's funny to think that, before the quake, it was challenge and adventure that my friends, Shelley, and I had sought to enrich our lives, to escape the normality of everyday-ness. Thanks to the earthquake, we had been thrown headfirst into them, and with no end in sight.

Two weeks later, the death toll was still rising as more bodies were found in the rubble. I hadn't been back into the centre of the city but heard from others that large portions of it were inaccessible. The latest estimate was that half of Christchurch would have to be rebuilt. Luckily, our house was liveable, though it too would need to be demolished at some stage. It was likely all ten houses in our lane would go, along with thousands of others spread throughout the city.

Power finally came back on in our street, and our day-to-day living at least started to feel a little more normal. But most of the eastern district resembled a ghost town. Tens of thousands of residents had already left Christchurch to find solace in other parts of New Zealand, and to get away from the growing number of aftershocks.

Where to from here? I had no idea, but at least we were alive and uninjured. So many families and friends had lost someone they'd cared for. And hundreds of others were in the hospital with serious injuries. Christchurch—and life—would never be the same. But how could they be after a natural disaster of that magnitude?

Luckily for Jamie and Jess, their house had coped well in the quakes. But Marty's home, like ours, sustained considerable damage.

'Things are still pretty unsettling,' Marty said, laughing, when I called around one afternoon for coffee. Another aftershock had us momentarily considering which doorframe to shelter under.

Once the room had settled, Marty continued: 'We are comfortable enough in our house and feel the rhythm coming back. At least we've got a roof over our heads, not like a lot of others. So we're lucky in that sense. But it's not a fun experience, not knowing when the next bomb's going to hit.'

Possibly because we were outdoor enthusiasts— experienced with making decisions about risk, eating basic food, using gas cookers, or digging a hole in the ground for a toilet—our other friends, neighbours, and family members looked to us for help, direction, and, possibly, a sense of calmness. Responding to natural challenges was something that came easily enough to us. And so, for the time being, the important challenges and adventures were focussed in our own backyard.

'I'm not leaving without the cats,' Shelley said after the radio announcer had warned of a potential tsunami.

The sudden alert wasn't because of our earthquakes; rather, Japan had just experienced its own devastating series of offshore shakes, and parts of the New Zealand coastline were also deemed in the firing line of a potential tidal wave.

Nothing eventuated. But, watching live televised footage of huge tsunamis sweeping through the coastal settlements in Japan and devastating everything in their path certainly heightened our own anxieties. At one stage, seeing the carnage unfold on television brought me to tears.

Royce, one of our elderly neighbours who lived on his own, came over mid-morning for a cup of tea.

'I just don't want to be alone,' he'd said quietly, sitting in our kitchen and sipping Earl Grey.

Days after catching up with Royce, we still hadn't seen much of our cats Tommy and George. Each new series of aftershocks had sent them scurrying to well-considered bolt holes. Sometimes I'd wished I could follow, lock myself away from the world and just breathe in the darkness.

The ground was no longer a steady, reliable thing. It continued to shake. There were over ten thousand aftershocks; even weeks later, we were still counting. I couldn't decide whether to put valuables back on shelves and desks or leave them on the floor. Surfboards were placed strategically for a worst-case scenario of a sudden tidal wave sweeping through our neighbourhood.

There was still no running water, and the city's sewerage system was in tatters. We used a hole in the backyard until the council finally delivered port-a-loos to the street. Effluent from the treatment system poured into the ocean.

There is no balance to nature. It ebbs and flows like the tide. And the irony is that we, as a society, had brought our inability to cope upon ourselves. It wasn't because of the earthquake; rather, it was how reliant we'd become on things, how comfortable we'd tried to make ourselves. I'm not saying that this attitude is right or wrong, but more that the difference in our capability becomes apparent when basic necessities are suddenly taken away.

Ironically, the western side of Christchurch—the affluent

side—was largely unaffected by the quakes and carried on like normal. The residents there complained about having to fix minute cracks in their driveways as if to make them feel a part of this.

Meanwhile, in the east, we tried to stop the rain from getting in by plugging a six-inch-wide gap torn through the concrete pad of our home with towels. The really poor suburbs nearby were the last to get chemical toilets delivered. I thought this kind of attitude had disappeared decades ago. The divide between the haves and the have-nots never seemed so vast.

Months passed. On one chilly day, while looking out the window of our upstairs bedroom, I watched heavy, wet snowflakes coat Christchurch in a blanket of white. Winter had well and truly fallen from the sky, plummeting temperatures and locking down much of the city with frozen or flooded streets.

In a way, the depths of winter masked the continuing drag of life post-earthquake. Snow hid the craters in the road and softened the sharp edges of broken buildings. There was still little need for an alarm clock, early morning aftershocks doing the trick. Shelley and I lay in bed in the half-light, trying to find the motivation to get up and turn the coffee machine on, knowing that, soon after the first cup, we would have to make the long, cold trudge to the nearest portable toilet in the street. At least it was covered, rather than our emergency hole in the backyard.

My mind drifted again to climbing. I couldn't wait to get back into the hills. After all of the risk and stress in the city, it felt like a relief to finally think about planning a trip to the mountains. To a place where, hopefully, things would be simpler, or at least make more sense.

NINE

The mountain might have seemed one of the less inspiring peaks in the Hopkins Valley but, somehow, I managed to convince Shelley and a friend, Graham Zimmerman, to explore a nondescript, frozen recess in one of the gullies below Rabbiters Peak. It was the winter of 2011. If nothing else, any escape from post-earthquake life in Christchurch was a good enough reason.

In summer, a waterfall at the recess nourishes Mount Cook lilies, buttercups and snow tussock. Its presence encourages tahr to shelter on the shoulders of nearby rock outcrops, all the time continuing its erosion into the earth. But, through the bleakest months, the fall of water becomes suspended. It grows into an icy streak whose heart remains mostly unnoticed within the eastern folds of Rabbiters.

Over the years, many other climbers would have headed towards more obvious features further up the valley, perhaps never giving the recess a glance. Never seeing enough to want to enquire further. To explore. As the seasons passed, the waterfall would thaw and refreeze undisturbed.

Even for me, the prospect of a decent climb here was an afterthought. Something that had barely caught my attention on an earlier trip. At best, a *maybe*. But, because of an approaching storm, Shelley, Graham, and I decided not to commit to anything requiring more time. The nor'wester had arrived. We figured on getting one day of okay weather and no more.

Monument Hut shuddered like there was an earthquake. Then, silence in the early morning darkness. Then another shake. Even though I knew it was only the wind, a part of me couldn't help but flinch and look for somewhere to shelter.

The hut was surrounded on three sides by beech forest. Wind from the northwest only reached it in gusts, accelerating into the lee and then retreating like it knew it was a thief. Or a harbinger.

Outside, the most elderly beech trees groaned and complained through an insipid dawn. There was the crash of a snapping branch. *Maybe we should just pack our gear and get out of here*, I thought. But, no. Shelley was already up and about, and Graham cheekily called for coffee from his sleeping bag. That overly protective part of my mind that constantly searches for reasons not to allowed itself a long, begrudging sigh of acceptance.

For some reason, while still walking up the steep hill from Monument Hut towards Rabbiters Peak, I had volunteered to lead the first pitch of the climb. Those who know me know I can be a terrible starter in the mountains. Sometimes my nerves get the better of me, doubts intensifying to a point where I just want to go home. Only once I'm absorbed by the intricacies of the climb do my nerves usually fall away.

I can't remember why I'd said to the others that I wanted to go first. But, as I started to tie into my harness at the base of the now rather intimidating frozen gully beneath Rabbiters, I was certainly regretting it.

Shelley watched me. Then she quietly stepped forward, placed her hands over mine and reached to take the ropes.

'I'll do it, Paul. If you like. You can lead the next pitch.'

I looked at her, then up at the ice. 'Are you sure?'

My wife nodded. 'I need to get moving. To warm up,' she added, trying to make out it was me doing her a favour rather than the other way around. 'My fingers are starting to get cold.'

I studied the route for a few more moments. What had seemed quite short from the valley now appeared to be a longer, much more challenging undertaking. The ice rose in tiers, following the same course that the water took in the warmer months. The rock on either side was steep; in some places it was overhanging, covered in icicles that looked like chandelier crystals, or upside-down daggers, depending on your state of mind first thing in the morning, in the middle of winter, with a storm approaching.

I took a deep breath, smiled at Shelley, and gladly handed her the ropes.

We were ascending the lee of the mountain, sheltered from the wind, moving under clouds that were continuing to bear down. Everything carried a patina of grey. My doubts slipped away as I began to climb after Shelley, the mood of the weather forgotten about. I'd managed to sniff out decent ice close to a hut and, by the looks of it, we would all get our turn at the sharp end of the rope. *Yeah, we are climbing!*

For me, climbing ice is as much about sound and feel as it is about sight. While I'm studying the colour and texture of the ice, and scanning for cracks across its surface after I imbed each tool, I'm also listening to the noise it makes. Is there a *thunk* or a *tink*? Does the ice sound compact or hollow? Can I feel a reverberation back through the handle of my ice axe? Is my placement solid? These details provide an intricate, necessary map in my mind. They dictate how and in which direction I will choose to climb.

'Nice lead,' I said to Shelley after joining her at the top of the first pitch.

'I reckon. Good effort,' Graham added.

Shelley shrugged her shoulders. 'Would have preferred to get another screw in before that bulge.' Then she grinned. 'Right, who's next?'

We all looked up. The ice gully narrowed, but appeared more easily angled than what we had just ascended. *Definitely time for me to take the lead!*

'Reckon I might solo this bit,' Graham said while I was re-looping extendable quickdraws and racking screws onto my harness.

'No worries, mate,' I replied. 'Whatever you feel like.'

Graham was a particularly strong climber, especially on ice, and I figured he could manage most of the route without much added risk to himself. Giving the thumbs up to Shelley, I started climbing while my friend was still deciding.

I have never asked Graham what it was that made him choose to stay tied into the rope, but that decision saved his life.

The ice before me submitted like softened plastic. Each swing of my tools and kick from my crampons sunk deeply and securely without much effort. But, soft ice meant unreliable protection.

High above, to the left, a wall of dark rock rose skywards. *Maybe there is a crack in it where I can wedge a nut. Or the ice nearby might be thicker and firmer, strong enough for screws.* Glancing down, I realised the others were now out of sight beyond a twist in the gully, and I estimated that the end of the ropes must be getting close.

Spindrift floated like frozen tears around me as I climbed, some of it sliding off my helmet to trickle down the back of my neck. I imagined the mountain to be crying. *Sorry to disturb you. We'll be gone soon.*

Climbing is about staying attuned to all of the particulars that a landscape hints at, whether it be frozen tears or softened ice. This is especially true when the way forward is unknown. For me, there is always a calculation of what this means, of what might be possible.

I kicked a small ledge in frozen snow beneath the rock wall. It was a decent enough stance, sheltered from the main ice runnel and with almost enough space for the three of us. Above, the ice pinched between two flanges of rock. Then it rose in a long, vertical sheet. *That will be Graham's lead!*

I ran my gloved hands across the surface of the rock, brushing away a veneer of snow and searching for imperfections. There were no cracks, the rock a shield. The ice beneath my tools also seemed too fragile, so the only option was to shuffle back to the middle of the gut. This would be more exposed to falling debris, especially when the others were climbing above me, but it was the only place for a reliable belay. I unclipped one of the screws from my harness and started twisting it into the ice.

Winter climbing, even at its meekest, is still a form of masochism. There may be moments of flow, but there are also moments of *Fuck this, it's cold!* By now, the tips of my fingers and toes were numb. My nose was running, and sometimes the drips of mucus froze before I had a chance to wipe them clear. I relaxed each calf in turn, trying to ease the tension from the front points of my crampons, then reset the grip of my left hand on the ice axe while, with my right, I kept turning the screw to its hilt. My focus was on the screw, on creating security for myself and the others.

A few minutes later, I had finished securing a second screw and tied myself to both of them. I was satisfied; finally, I was safe from what would otherwise be a very long tumble. I began to pull in the slack from the ropes to set up a belay so the others could climb. Then the ice fell.

The next moments have replayed over and over in my mind. The impact. The violence. Thinking about it now, I can still vividly recall the sensation of what felt like a skip-full of bricks being tipped upon my head. There was no surge of fear or wondering whether it was finally *the* moment. I just collapsed with the force, slumping against the screws. Falling ice kept thumping onto me. Then everything went black.

Had I missed something? A hidden detail that could have helped avert disaster? Even now, the risk assessor in me can't let it go, another *what if* to file away, a weight some climbers seem to carry easily in their psyche, while others—the ones whose judgment I have learned to trust—consider it a burden of responsibility.

I don't think I was unconscious for very long, maybe only a few seconds. I tried to fight the fogginess in my mind, to become aware again. Wiping my face, I realised it was blood, not sweat, in my eyes. There was pain across my head and shoulders. My left hand couldn't grip. My ribs throbbed each time I tried to breathe. *Don't shy away from the pain*, I told myself. *Focus on it. Use it.* I was alive. I just hoped that Shelley and Graham were, too.

I leaned out and shouted down, but then figured the others probably wouldn't hear me over the noise of the wind. My self-control was threatening to unravel. *How badly has the ice hit them? Are they hurt? Stop thinking that!* Of course, there was no use worrying about what might have happened. I needed to get down to see what *had* happened.

Aware of only having full use of my right hand, and that dropping the ropes now would likely finish what the falling ice had started, I took extra, precious minutes getting ready to abseil to the others, and to any hope of safety.

Mountaineering accidents tend to be either minor or fatal, and this was something in between. Ten seconds earlier and I wouldn't have been clipped to the anchors; when the ice had fallen, I would have gone the distance, quite possibly pulling Graham and Shelley's anchor, too. *Forget that*, I told myself. *Focus on what is happening. Keep moving. Get down. Deal with whatever challenge gets in the way.*

I took a glance back up, above my anchor, trying to work out where the ice had detached from. More could fall any second. *Just get the hell out of here!*

It seemed like a lifetime, but was likely less than half a minute, before I had descended enough to see Shelley and Graham. They were still there. Still anchored at their belay. The relief made me want to cry. *All of us, we are alive!*

My eyes met Shelley's. At least her belay stance meant that she had been off to one side of the gully, partially sheltered from the full force of the falling ice. I gave thanks to a deity I don't believe in that she hadn't been the one leading the second pitch.

'Are you okay?' I asked.

She nodded awkwardly. I couldn't see any physical injuries other than bloody scrapes on her face, and she was still on her feet.

Graham looked much worse. He had been preparing to climb, and it was likely he'd copped the impact of the icefall directly, like I had. Of course, the ice had fallen much farther to reach him, all the time accelerating down the gully, so it could only have been more awful for him.

My friend initially didn't respond to the sound of my voice. He stayed slumped in the snow, looking down and cradling one arm with the other.

'How you doing, Zim?...*Graham?*'

He finally replied, 'My shoulder's fucked. And my leg—I think it might be broken, too.'

I took a deep breath, which hurt like hell but helped refocus my thinking. A broken leg meant Graham couldn't walk. I was having enough trouble moving on my own, and now I was going to have to help him. I remember telling myself *small steps*, trying to break down what suddenly seemed another huge issue. Then, I allowed a wry smile. We were all broken; taking small steps was exactly what we would be doing.

Partway up an ice climb was no place to assess Graham's injuries any further.

'No worries, mate,' I said, trying to sound positive. 'How about we get you to the ground, and then we can go from there?'

I ran through various scenarios in my head as I lowered Graham. Even though the wind had increased, I could hear him mumbling to himself, telling himself whatever he needed to keep moving. My friend was doing what he had to to get through this. We all were.

Although it was a shitty situation, I couldn't think of better people to be with. We would fight as hard as we could for each other for as long as we breathed.

'Are you okay if I abseil down next?' I asked Shelley. She took a glance up at the gully, worrying about more ice falling.

'If I go first, I can tie up Graham's shoulder and do a quick assessment of him as you come down. Maybe even start helping him to the hut.'

'Okay,' she said. 'That makes sense. What about the PLB?'

I had a personal locator beacon in my pack. So far, I had refrained from setting it off. The most important thing to do first was to get ourselves off the mountain, out of the firing line of any more ice.

'Let's get to the hut,' I reasoned. 'Then we can make a decision about what to do next.'

Monument Hut was an obvious target. There, we had shelter and food. Barring more ice falling on us, or the onset of hypothermia, no one was going to die. Once at the hut, the storm could do what it wanted and we would still be safe.

The ropes went slack, which meant Graham had reached the ground. I threaded my abseil device and gave Shelley a gentle hug before continuing my descent.

'I reckon I can walk,' Graham said once I'd reached him.

'What's that?' I asked, wondering if I had heard him correctly.

'My leg. It must be the fibula that's broken. I think I can walk on it. At least try.'

I glanced dubiously at his leg, at the same time trying to recall my limited knowledge of lower limb anatomy. But Graham seemed adamant. I helped him to his feet and gave him my hiking pole.

'Okay, mate, just take it quietly. We'll be right behind you.

If it gets too much, just sit down and wait for us. Um...Try not to fall over.'

Graham grimaced at my attempted humour. 'You think?'

I watched my friend shuffle across the snow-covered boulders and scree. He tried a few different techniques, holding the pole at various heights, before settling on one where he could make progress downhill with the least amount of pain. I'd climbed with Graham enough times over the years to know how reliable he was and how determined he could be. In his mind, he had set a goal of reaching the hut, and he was definitely going to get there.

'Where's Graham?' Shelley asked once she had abseiled to where I was waiting.

'He reckoned he could walk.'

'Really?'

'I know, right? Let's see how far he gets.'

I took the ropes from Shelley. Trying to minimise the pain in my ribs, I started pulling them down.

My wife turned to me. 'What do you think we should do?'

I checked down the hill to judge Graham's progress. 'He's going fine by the looks. Once we catch up, can you help him to the hut if he needs it?'

'Okay.'

'I reckon best thing might be for me to carry on ahead. Change into my walking shoes and head out to the road.'

'Why not use the PLB?'

'Do you think we should?'

Shelley shrugged her shoulders.

'It'll take a fair while for anyone to get organised and travel in to us,' I reasoned, as much to myself as Shelley. 'I can be out in a couple of hours, get to the car and find a local farmer with a four-wheel drive. They'll get in here no worries, and then we can drive ourselves to the hospital. It'll be quicker, I reckon.'

Shelley and I started walking down after Graham. 'If I head out, at least we know that something is happening rather than just sitting around and waiting,' I said to Shelley. 'With the storm coming, any rescuers might not get in here for ages.'

I've thought about my decision-making process many times since that day. Was seeking help on my own the right thing to do, or should I have activated the PLB? I have always had a philosophy of trying to self-rescue as much as possible. The three of us were injured, but no one was going to die. While we could, I figured we should be doing everything possible to keep ourselves safe. This was not out of any notion of being tough, but rather a sense of personal responsibility. And, maybe if I'm totally honest now, a streak of stubbornness. Of finishing what we'd started.

Graham and Shelley had almost reached Monument Hut by the time I was about to leave it. It was unexpectedly difficult to remove my broken helmet; it had all but fused to the wound on the top of my head. A good yank and a fair amount of swearing finally did the trick. I popped some painkillers from my kit at the hut, left the remainder on the table where Shelley and Graham would see them, and headed out the door.

More than once during the walk to the road's end, I cursed myself for not relenting and setting off the PLB. The adrenaline from dealing with the immediate aftermath of the icefall and getting everyone down had worn off; now I was just left with the drudgery of walking with a sore head and a nagging pain in my ribs.

There was no one home at the first farm I checked. But I managed to wave down a father and son who were driving to the nearby Temple Valley for a hunting trip. Once I had explained the situation, they were more than happy to help, and their shiny four-wheel drive easily handled the rough track to Monument Hut.

They dropped us back at our vehicle at the end of the road, and we then started the long drive to Christchurch Hospital. Shelley had said she was feeling better and had volunteered to do the driving. It was a relief to just sit there in the passenger seat, to be able to finally relax for a bit.

I called Jamie to fill him on on what had happened.

'Bro, you probably don't want to go to the hospital here,' he said.

'What? Why not?'

'I just heard on the news there was a big freeze overnight in the city. Apparently, the hospital is overflowing with slip victims from all the ice. Carnage by the sounds of it.'

'Shit, really?'

'Yeah. I reckon you guys might be better off going to Timaru instead. It's closer anyway, isn't it?'

It was late in the evening by the time we reached Timaru. We decided to stop for food *before* going to the hospital—well, Graham and Shelley had demanded, and I'd acquiesced. The three of us stood in the queue at Burger King, smeared in dried blood and with down jackets torn, trying to look inconspicuous enough so that the staff would actually take our order rather than call the police.

Later, the nurse at the hospital cracked jokes about my 'hard noggin' as he pulled hair from the wound with tweezers and then glued the gash back together. The duty doctor said there wasn't much point in X-raying my ribs as the treatment was the same regardless of whether they were cracked or just bruised. She also took some convincing to X-ray Graham's lower leg after he'd explained how far he had managed to hobble on it.

'If you walked on it, I don't believe it's broken,' she insisted.

'I reckon it might be,' Graham replied, trying to be patient.

'No. I don't think so.'

I could see that my friend was getting frustrated. 'Look, can you please just X-ray it?' he said. 'Then we'll know for sure, either way.'

Finally, the doctor agreed. And, yes, it was broken.

Shelley and I were discharged that night, but Graham's injuries meant he had to remain in the hospital. We found a cheap motel nearby, but I couldn't sleep. My body ached all over and my mind wouldn't quit replaying the day. *Fuck, that was close. Too close!* I think it was only the quiet sound of Shelley's breathing—a positive reminder of the outcome—that finally allowed me to relax.

The falling ice did a good job on Graham's shoulder. The top of his scapula had been broken in two, and it was recommended he stay another night so a specialist could assess whether immediate surgery was required.

Shelley and I left Graham in the main ward next to another patient: a boisterous young man with a very short haircut who'd said he wanted to take up climbing and then had demanded to know all the details from our accident. It felt like we were deserting Graham to his new 'friend'.

To pass the time, we went to the local movie theatre to watch *The Green Lantern* and then spent the latter part of the day trying to find accommodation for a second night. Apparently, a big sports tournament was in town over the weekend and every motel we visited was fully booked.

Luckily, at our last option, there was a sudden vacancy

because a commercial flight had been cancelled due to the weather. Hearing our story, the receptionist even reduced the rate for what ended up being more of a flash apartment than a motel room.

My cellphone rang around the same time we were thinking about dinner. It was Graham.

'Can you guys come and get me?'

'Are you allowed out?' I asked.

'No, not really. But this dude is driving me crazy.'

Half an hour later, the three of us were back at the motel, sitting in front of the television with takeaways. Graham had taken a good supply of painkillers, so was particularly happy, and we joked about any repercussions from breaking him out of the hospital.

Then, we heard what sounded like a key in the lock of the front door. In walked the pilot from the supposedly cancelled flight, which had actually only been postponed. To his credit, the pilot apologised for the misunderstanding and promptly left again. But we wondered whether our accommodation was secure.

A few minutes later, the phone rang.

'Here we go,' I said. 'This will be the motel guy kicking us out.'

But it wasn't. It was a nurse from the hospital asking whether we had Graham and that, if so, could we please promptly return him.

Not surprisingly, the accident affected my motivation to go back to the mountains, but I still managed to return with Jamie two months later to finish the climb. Jamie kindly offered to lead every pitch. My hands shook for most of the ascent, and I couldn't help double-checking each anchor and every single swing of my ice axes. I found myself constantly looking up, wondering what else waited unseen, not just on this climb, but at any stage of my life. How could I make good decisions to protect myself and others against something I didn't even know existed?

We called the climb Honey Badger. Inspiration for the name came from a video we had watched of a honey badger fighting cobras. It seemed appropriate for this piece of anonymous country that had almost taken Shelley, Graham, and me; the three of us had been bitten by the snaking ice, but we'd managed to survive.

I guess it's no surprise that I couldn't relax until both ropes were pulled after the final abseil, and we were well clear of any chance of falling ice. Jamie and I stood and looked back up at what we had just climbed.

Jamie yelled out, 'Honey badger don't give a shit'—a quote from the video. Then, we descended from Rabbiters Peak.

TEN

Live or die. For us, a few seconds had made all the difference. There were so many *what ifs* to consider. What if I hadn't clipped the anchor in time? What if Shelley and I hadn't swapped leads? What if Graham hadn't tied into the rope?

I reflected on aspects of the climb and the accident for a long time afterwards. Part of it was probably dealing with the shock, but even more so, it was about learning from the experience and then trying to put what had happened into perspective. Climbing is about having fun, but it's also about managing risk or avoiding it wherever possible. And, I guess, that's the mental crux: when does the risk become too high?

We were lucky. Bloody lucky! Sure, perhaps we were unlucky to get hit by the ice. But the results could have been so much worse.

Talking to Graham afterwards about the climb, he suggested that perhaps we shouldn't have committed to the ice gully.

'Anything falling was going to get funnelled towards us,' he reasoned.

'But that's where the good ice was,' I replied. 'If we wanted to climb the route, we had to be in the gully.'

'That's it in a nutshell, don't you think?' he said. 'Our focus was too much on what we *wanted*. The only way to be safe was to not be in there in the first place. I'm sure we could have found something else to climb that wasn't so dangerous.'

I understood where Graham was coming from, but then what he was referring to could be said for any climbing, or indeed any other risky activity. We didn't realise beforehand how dangerous our climb might be. It's a fine thing, trying to judge how much risk on a particular mountaineering trip is appropriate.

Australian climber and author Greg Child has written about this topic. Child believes that climbers tend to rely on 'a capricious and often flawed instinct' to sway between what he terms 'recklessness and calculated risk'. He calls this rationalisation a thin line of reason.

While Child was referring to professional mountaineering, it is also true that the seriousness of any situation depends largely on our choices beforehand, previous experience, constant reassessment and then the actions we take. How often have I felt the need to scramble across an avalanche-prone gully against my better judgement? Or move beneath a creaking cornice? Necessity has forced me to take a risk, perhaps to avoid an even greater risk later.

The reality is that the consequences of risk are only comprehended when something goes wrong. As climbers, we read or hear about accidents involving other climbers, and we hope that they never happen to us. We have to hope this, but it's the extent to which we let this hope cloud our judgement that can affect the outcome.

How do I put this experience into a wider perspective, one that might make sense to climbers and non-climbers alike? As American author and activist Edward Abbey once wrote: 'A venturesome minority will always be eager to set off on their own, and no obstacles should be placed in their path; let them take risks, for godsake, let them get lost, sunburnt, stranded, drowned, eaten by bears, buried alive under avalanches—that is the right and privilege of any free [person].'

Abbey had a point. There are always going to be adrenaline junkies and risk takers. They can decide to do what they want because of freedom of choice. It's their prerogative to endanger themselves. And while not wanting to support recklessness, accepting that risk has a place in our lives—that it adds value—is a good thing.

Modern society, New Zealand's included, is becoming increasingly risk-averse. A friend, Chris North, who has worked as a lecturer in outdoor and environmental education at the University of Canterbury, feels quite strongly about this topic.

'This obsession with more and more safety is one of our social panics,' Chris once said to me. 'Risk is seen as something we need to protect our children from, rather than teach them how to deal with. Yet this comes at a time when the children of our generation are safer than they've ever been.'

While recognising that any outdoor activity has a certain level of danger, Chris believes that there is too much focus on avoiding all risk, especially concerning the outdoor education of our youth. 'We are missing the point by having such a narrow focus on the potential consequences, rather than all of the possible benefits,' my friend said. 'The feeling of achievement and connection that comes from participating in these types of activities can make us better able to deal with daily pressures back home. They help to put everything in perspective.'

Like Chris, I believe that the skills and experiences gained from outdoor activity add value to our wider lives, and as a result, the outdoors provide great learning opportunities for our youth. 'Outdoor experience isn't a panacea, but used in the right context, it may help teenagers through their difficult years,' Chris said to me. 'Concepts like responsibility and consequence become apparent, helping make the transition to adulthood easier.'

Chris, a 'former mountaineer and wannabe mountain biker', hopes that society doesn't continue to head down the road of being overly cautious. 'We've become so fixated on the risk in outdoor education that we've forgotten all the other benefits connected with it,' he said. 'Matching competence against challenges is a recognised way of learning and personal growth. Spending time in nature is also a way to build connections to the world beyond humanity, and realise we are part of something bigger. Within this context, outdoor recreation can be powerful, and a healthy avenue for those looking for challenge.'

Like Greg Child, Chris also recognises and accepts that there is a fine line to how much risk is appropriate. 'In education, if you are putting people into situations that have higher levels of risk, there needs to be sound educational principles behind the reasoning for it,' he explained. 'The point of an outdoor experience is not the risk itself, but the rewards that come with the experience. And, while too much risk is unacceptable, the elimination of risk is impossible and, I firmly believe, undesirable.'

From my perspective, the right level of exposure to risk is a personal decision. What's right for me may not be right for someone else.

Let's explore this perception of risk from a different view. I recently watched the movie *North face* during a local film festival. The movie tells the true story of an ill-fated 1936 attempt on Switzerland's notorious 1700-metre-high Eiger North Wall. Bavarians Andreas Hinterstoisser and Toni Kurz were in a race with Austrians Eduard Rainer and Willy Angerer to be the first to ascend the face. Others had already died attempting the climb, either hit by rockfall or caught out in deteriorating weather.

What struck me most about the movie was the contrast between the immediate challenges and increasing dangers faced by the climbers, and the detached, almost sadistic, attitude of the public watching from below. As is often the case with armchair critics, the voyeurs showed great delight in judging certain actions without any understanding of what was actually occurring, and then took an almost 'I told you so' attitude when tragedy struck.

To my way of thinking, not much has changed in the seventy or so years since then. Climbers still head out and pit themselves against the terrain and the elements. Those who stay behind, who choose not to fill their lives with such action, are still quick to judge others when things go wrong.

As a climber, I cringe when the general news media comes up with headlines like 'Killer Mountain' or 'Trapped in the Death Zone'. Journalists focus on the thrill and danger of mountaineering without attempting to give it any sense of perspective. Sometimes, I feel defensive when an interviewed member of the police force or rescue service states that so-and-so didn't carry enough equipment or make the right decisions.

This is the problem with hindsight: looking back, it is

easier to see the timeline of events—what went right and what went wrong—but in the heat of the moment, these factors are not always apparent. And I guess that was the case with our accident on Rabbiters. Despite our combined experience and assessment, we still didn't account for the possibility of ice falling from above. Sometimes shit just happens.

ELEVEN

John Lennon once said, 'Life is what happens to you while you're busy making other plans.' Earthquakes. Climbing accidents. Car crashes. Terminal illness. None of these things are planned for, but they happen. Being able to deal with the stress of the unexpected comes with learning from different experiences. And one of my greatest learning experiences was a mountaineering expedition to Pakistan.

When well-meaning family and friends heard about my planned trip, the conversation went something like this: 'You want to go where? The place with all the bombings? Aren't they beheading westerners? Why in God's name would you want to go there?'

Why, indeed? As others tried to dissuade me from accepting my friend Pat Deavoll's invite to join her, I found myself increasingly drawn to the idea. This was despite all of the negative western media. I'd watch news reports of increasing conflict between the Pakistan Armed Forces and the Taliban, and hints that the Pakistani government and country were on the verge of collapse. As I could only try to separate the facts from whatever slant the American or English reporters had decided on, I didn't understand what was really happening in the fundamentalist Muslim country. I felt ignorant, something easily experienced from our safe haven down here in the Southern Pacific.

Pat had travelled to and climbed in Pakistan on a number of occasions, including the two previous years, and she agreed that the risk this time around was probably higher. Still, life is about putting yourself out there from time to time, and the more I researched the country and its people, the more fascinated I became. The combination of geographical contrasts, and even the political edginess, convinced me that I needed to experience it for myself. I had travelled to both India and Kyrgyzstan for mountaineering expeditions the previous two years, and was keen to compare the differences—and the mountains—between the three countries. Travelling through Pakistan would be a different kind of risk, one that I would have to try to understand and then, hopefully, manage.

The goal for the trip was a 6180-metre unclimbed mountain called Karim Sar, located near the Hunza Valley in Pakistan's Gilgit-Baltistan Area. Pat had spotted the mountain during one of her previous trips, and she'd found out that it had been attempted unsuccessfully by a strong Italian team. Apart from that, we didn't know much about the mountain or the Shutinbar Valley we were planning to approach it from. The Italians wouldn't divulge any information as they were keen to head back for another go.

To reach Karim Sar, we needed to travel along the fabled

Karakoram Highway (KKH) first to the city of Gilgit, and then on to Chalt, and finally the small settlement of Budelas. Part of the road trip meant squeezing between the eastern fringes of the Swat District, where the Taliban and Pakistan military were still fighting, and the constantly troubled Kashmir border between Pakistan and India. Along with occasional suicide bombings in various urban areas, and of course the actual climbing, this was likely to be the riskiest part of the journey.

'How do you know when it isn't safe?' I asked Baig, our local guide, after he'd met us at Islamabad Airport. Heavily armed military personnel and police officers patrolled the airport's entrance, perimeter, and surrounding roads.

'It is always safe, until you meet bad people,' he replied. 'Then, very quickly, it isn't safe anymore.'

Baig worked for Nazir Sabir Expeditions, the company we were using to organise all of our logistics in Pakistan. Company owner Nazir Sabir was a famous high-altitude climber known for having achieved a difficult first ascent on K2, Pakistan's highest mountain and the second-highest mountain in the world behind Mount Everest.

In previous years, Nazir Sabir Expeditions had organised many trips, but more recently there had been a sharp drop in the number of western tourists wanting to visit. Baig partially blamed the western media for creating a false impression about the dangers of travel in his country. He explained that, while certain areas were considered dangerous, westerners could usually still travel unhindered.

I found Baig's comments to be in contrast to the way the company limited Pat and my attempts at unsupervised sightseeing in Islamabad, nearby Rawalpindi, and, later, parts of the KKH. Understandably, they were cautious, because if something did happen to us, it would no doubt damage what little business remained for Nazir Sabir Expeditions.

Pat and I remained in Islamabad for two days while getting our freighted luggage through customs—and then trying to locate the handful of items missing when it did arrive. After flying out from a bleak New Zealand winter, the 40+ degree Celsius temperature proved somewhat combative. We limited our supervised sightseeing to short bursts, spending the remainder of our time in air-conditioned hotel rooms.

Islamabad was a clean and organised city. Apart from the numerous concrete barriers and security checks to dissuade suicide bombings, traffic flowed smoothly along well-maintained roads lined with trees and grass verges. Traffic police—some looking surprisingly like Erik Estrada from the 1980s television show *CHiPs*—kept their eye on speedsters and dangerous drivers.

This was almost the exact opposite to the hustle and hassle we'd see in Rawalpindi. Convergence, a keen judgement of nonexistent gaps, and horns kept traffic inching in various directions. This was part of why I liked to venture to these kinds of places. Perhaps due to the accepted chaos, a certain vitality existed here, something that the more restrictive rules back in New Zealand didn't allow for. There's something satisfying about being able to sit on the horn because the vehicle in front is travelling too slow, pulling out to pass regardless of what traffic is coming the other way, and leaving the onus on the driver that caused the initial slowdown to avoid any ensuing vehicular carnage.

This optimistic approach was exhibited wholeheartedly by our soft-spoken driver, Wali Khan, as he navigated the dusty and winding KKH to Budelas. Wali's relationship with the edge of the road, not to mention the possible plummet beyond it to the Indus River hundreds of metres below, encouraged me to look up at the surrounding countryside rather than focus too much on his driving. The irony that our cause of death—rather than being from the danger of the Taliban or climbing a mountain—could be the enthusiasm of Wali Khan to get us to our destination as quickly as possible, was not lost on me.

Towns and settlements flashed past. Some were deemed too unsafe to stop at due to the likelihood of insurgents harbouring there. We spent three hours in a queue at Mansehra, waiting to cross what was left of a bridge that had been partially blown up the night before by Islamic militants. Heading the other way were scores of trucks loaded with refugees trying to escape the fighting in Swat. Forced from their villages by either the Pakistan military or the Taliban, they had travelled in tens of thousands over Shangla Pass, heading to specially established camps near Islamabad. In all, more than a million residents were displaced from their homes by the fighting.

Seeing the effects firsthand made me realise, not for the first time, how easy we had it in New Zealand, and how we tended to take our liberty for granted. The daily struggle for even basic necessities was very real and, at times, desperate for a majority of Pakistanis. And this was while western democracy sat on the sidelines, judging a religion and a culture it didn't fully understand. Small wonder, then, that certain factions turned against the west with such ferocity.

We spent a night in what felt like a deserted tourist district in Chilas. Chilas was the closest city to the impressive 8126-metre-high mountain Nanga Parbat. One of only fourteen mountains over 8000 metres high in the world, Nanga Parbat has a notorious reputation as being dangerous to climb, especially its 4500-metre-high Rupal Face—the highest rock wall on any mountain in the world.

The next day, we stopped for lunch at a small roadside stall.

Baig was reading a local newspaper, and he told me about an article reporting that the Taliban had been trying to purchase children directly from poor families. The terrorists would train these children to become suicide bombers. Selling one child meant the rest of the family could be fed and housed safely. And there I was, spending thousands of dollars on an expedition that had no value other than a recreational pursuit of my own selfish desire.

At Budelas, we hired porters and donkeys for the two-day trek to Base Camp. During the walk in, I was surprised how quickly the crumbling silt escarpments of the lower Chalt district gave way to pockets of irrigated greenery. Cherries, mulberries, and apricots grew in abundance, and we followed the gentle uphill gradient of a long-established, stonewalled irrigation channel that somehow clung to the side of steep cliffs.

Above the cliffs, it took me some time to realise that I wasn't staring at steep-sided clouds. These were sheer, monstrous mountains, some with an elevation of five vertical kilometres from where we rested. They are among the most impressive testaments to alpine architecture that I have ever seen.

The world's three great mountain ranges converged here: the Himalaya, the Karakoram and the Hindu Kush. In these ranges, Pakistan has five mountains over 8000 metres high and more than one hundred over 7000 metres high. I couldn't even begin to comprehend the prolonged effort required to climb something so big.

At least Karim Sar was at a more modest altitude of 6180 metres. From our Base Camp, situated alongside the Shutinbar Glacier at around 3700 metres, the height seemed more in proportion to other climbs I had experienced in the past.

Pat and I settled into the slow routine of acclimatisation while scoping for a potential route through a threatening icefall that guarded access to Karim Sar. Afternoon thunderstorms and occasional snow showers kept us guessing about weather patterns. But, generally, any storm system tended not to last for very long.

A few days before we were going to attempt the climb on Karim Sar, I came down with a nose infection that affected my breathing and balance. I explained to Pat that I didn't feel strong or confident enough to leave camp until my symptoms had eased. I was surprised when this caused considerable conflict between us. Pat told me in no uncertain terms that she expected me to start the climb when she was ready, regardless of how I felt. Pat's negative attitude made me even more cautious; if she was this unsympathetic at Base Camp, I wondered what might happen during the actual climb.

This was a new experience for me. Managing the risk here wasn't just about what might happen on the mountain. It was also about a climbing partnership that didn't seem to be working. It felt like I couldn't rely on Pat the way I had been able to with my previous climbing partners. This perception may have been unfounded, and no doubt if I had been feeling healthy, then the conflict wouldn't likely have arisen in the first place. Perhaps it was me who needed to be more understanding towards the way that Pat was feeling.

Reflecting on this now, the fact that we were on a fully sponsored expedition may have twisted Pat's judgement. Her expectation might have been that, if necessary, we had to take more risk than we would have otherwise to satisfy the sponsors. Either way, I believed it was the right decision for me to remain at Base Camp until I felt well enough to look out for myself on the climb.

After four days on antibiotics, I still didn't feel healthy enough or, perhaps more accurately, confident enough to climb. But I agreed to help Pat as far up the mountain as I could. Over the next three days, we climbed back up through the icefall to establish a high camp. From there, Pat soloed the last 1000 metres to the summit while I waited, exhausted, at our 5200-metre tent site.

Given how I had been feeling, and the conflict I had encountered with Pat, I was happy to have made it that high. Thinking back, if Pat had been more of an understanding partner, I may have been prepared to try to climb further up the mountain. I had been starting to feel a bit better. But it didn't matter. Because of Pat's attitude, as well as my sickness, there was no way I was going to risk going higher. This was a new lesson for me, something that I noted in my mind so I would be better prepared if it happened again.

Pat returned successful from the summit. As we only had one sleeping bag at the high camp, I soloed back down the steep snow slope to our Advanced Base Camp tent site 1000 metres below. Pat joined me the following morning, and we retreated down through the icefall and out to Baig and our cook, Nisar, at Base Camp.

Instead of taking the riskier drive back along the Karakoram Highway, given that there were reports of more bombings, we managed to secure a flight out from the city of Gilgit to Islamabad. Gilgit has a heavy military presence, and amongst the passengers booked to fly to Islamabad was a large contingent of particularly well-dressed military personnel. I presumed they must all be high-ranking officers judging by the extensive, and very shiny, array of medals on display across their jackets.

Like many mountainous flights, the trip from Gilgit to

Islamabad seemed rather committing. The city is set near the end of a narrow valley and is flanked by high mountains on both sides. After taking off, it didn't look like aeroplanes had enough room to be able to return to the runway if necessary, and so had to continue to the end of the valley before making any turns.

On this day there were two flights, both twin turboprop ATRs or something similar, that were scheduled to leave close together. All of the generals boarded the first flight, and the rest of us were directed to the second. Our plane took off immediately behind the first plane and followed it down the valley. It seemed like our pilot needed to keep close to the first plane to know where to go, which I found rather amusing, and a tad unsettling. In terms of navigation, there weren't a lot of options. Take off, keep flying until you get to a really big mountain at the end of the valley and then turn right!

We flew past Nanga Parbat, but its astounding Rupal Face remained hidden from view. I tried to imagine myself partway up such a monstrous climb, dealing with the extreme level of commitment that would be required to attempt it. To be honest, and not surprisingly, it felt beyond me. I couldn't even imagine having the confidence to start.

TWELVE

Just as moving from the North Island's mountains to the south was a natural progression for me, so too was my growing desire to climb more overseas. I saw it as a new level of challenge. The peaks were higher. The risks were greater. There were more unknowns, including understanding the right way to interact with foreign cultures. The opportunity for exploration seemed endless.

Nearly all of New Zealand's top alpinists have chosen to head overseas at some stage. Perhaps they found themselves reaching a plateau here because our mountains simply aren't big enough, or they didn't have enough difficult routes within easy access. Achieving harder routes means constantly pushing one's limits across all facets of climbing. The best way to do this is probably in places such as the famed alpine resort of Chamonix in France or in the mountains of North America.

In New Zealand, there might only be one or two routes in

each recognised area that are at a technical enough standard for expert climbers. With somewhere like Chamonix, there are so many world-class routes right next to each other, and with easy access, that you can't help but get better at top-level climbing. Marty climbed overseas many times each year, and Jamie was also becoming drawn to the extra challenge offered by mountains with bigger reputations.

How many routes in New Zealand take longer than a day of actual climbing? There are hardly any south-facing ice routes here longer than around 10 pitches. On some technical routes overseas, you could be on the climb for four days—and on the Rupal Face of Nanga Parbat, even more than that. Kiwi climbers who don't head overseas miss out on that extended commitment factor.

I can understand why climbers want to head offshore. After eyeing up the monstrous faces on mountains in places like the Gangotri Valley of the Indian Himalaya, and in Pakistan, it can seem that even our longest and staunchest routes in the Southern Alps pale by comparison. Sure, there are some longer routes here, such as the Caroline Face of Aoraki / Mount Cook and the north ridge of Sefton (both with around 2000 metres of actual climbing as opposed to glacial walking), but their difficulty is in their length rather than any technical aspect. Most of the harder routes here involve less than 800 vertical metres of technical climbing—a height gain that can usually be ascended within a day.

Perhaps part of the problem with technical climbing in New Zealand is how we have graded our mountain routes. With only a single number given to demonstrate the overall difficulty of a route, the focus always seems to be on a crux grade, rather than acknowledging any extended difficulties. (This has since been rectified by editor Rob Frost leading the way in the latest version of the Aoraki Tai Poutini guidebook, and involves a multi-layered grading system that has been widely applauded).

For some, our mountains seem like they just aren't steep enough, hard enough, or high enough. They might be a great place to learn the ropes, so to speak, but if someone wants to be considered a world-class alpinist, then they need to travel and climb overseas, especially on technical mountains at a higher altitude.

However, some well-known and highly proficient Kiwi climbers would disagree with this assertion. Bill McLeod is considered one of our greatest mountaineers, someone noted for his solos of previously established climbs, as well as difficult new routes. Almost single-handedly, Bill reset the bar for technical alpinism in this country. But he never climbed overseas.

'I guess in my earlier years, when I was reading about Bonnington and Messner, there was an interest to climb overseas,' he once said to me. 'But when it came to spending the money, I'd rather have a new set of threads. I'd rather have a new pair of boots or axes or crampons. Why go to Everest and chug along behind some Sherpa when there's so much hard climbing to do in New Zealand? Once you've spent the money, what if the weather isn't right and you can't climb the mountain? You've got nothing. Here, if I can't get it this month, I'll get it next.'

Bill felt that, with enough exploration and perseverance, routes of extreme difficulty would continue to be found in the Southern Alps.

Allan Uren, another of our top alpinists, believed part of the issue around a lack of new hard routes was because there had been a drop-off in mountaineers trying to establish technical climbs in this country. 'Hard climbing in New Zealand was in the doldrums for quite a while,' he said.

Allan considered it a misconception that technical climbing only occurred overseas, and at a higher altitude. 'It's a shame,' he said. 'There's so much unclimbed stuff still to do in our mountains, some of it that could be quite challenging. I hope some of our next generation step up.'

In 2004, Allan made a first winter ascent of the northeast face of Torres Peak, near Mount Tasman, with Craig Jefferies. The 14 pitch route required two nights on the face in a bivouac bag and, according to Uren, involved 'insanely good technical climbing'. Perhaps this type of climb is the future for technical alpinism here—shortish routes of intense and prolonged difficulty.

Since Allan and Craig's climb, there has been a resurgence of harder routes in New Zealand's mountains. Perhaps encouraged by their example, a new generation of alpinists have searched for technical unclimbed terrain. And then, more recently, the emergence of the coronavirus has also forced climbers who might once have been motivated to climb overseas to instead focus on the opportunities that exist within our own shores.

As someone who has climbed extensively at home, as well as taking part in a number of expeditions abroad, I understand the appeal of both environments. While I've been lucky enough to complete first ascents here and overseas, I would consider myself a step below the level of technical difficulty that Bill and Allan were referring to. For me, climbing new routes is about taking on the unknown, rather than gunning for any specific technical difficulty. I get inspired by a mountain, or a face, or a line, and I try to climb it. If I end up getting more than I bargained for, then I just try to deal with that aspect of the climbing as best I can. It's only afterwards, when I can look back from the safety of my armchair, that I allow the 'shit, that was hard' factor to sink in. At the time, it's purely a matter of keeping moving and staying as safe as possible.

But then, it's human nature to allow that the more effort and commitment you put into something—especially something so difficult that it pushes you physically and mentally—then the greater the emotional response if you end up being successful. I've managed a couple of moderately difficult first ascents in New Zealand, and the intense feeling of commitment that I experienced on them, and then a strong sense of place afterwards, is something I'll always treasure.

Likewise, on my first overseas expedition, to Central Asia in 1996, as I approached the summit of our highest climb, I burst into tears. Maybe it was partly due to relief that I could turn around and go down, but that experience was one of the purest and strongest emotional responses to physical exertion in my life.

Obviously, there are much higher mountains overseas. If someone wants to keep increasing their level of commitment, then they are probably going to have to head to the Greater Ranges at some stage. But I can also relate to Allan's view that the potential connection with the spirit of a place is stronger in our own backyard. When I get amongst the Southern Alps, I feel a level of peace that is missing in the mountains overseas. And there is a history here, of the others who have gone before, as well as something I can perhaps contribute to.

Sometimes I want to push myself, and sometimes I want to just lie back and watch the clouds roll by, regardless of whether the location is in New Zealand or another country. The actual climbing is just part of a broader and more engaging experience.

Perhaps, one answer is to try for a longer expedition-type trip in New Zealand. To link specific climbs together by moving continuously between them. This would allow exploration of more remote corners in our mountains, along with the challenge of managing the logistics of climbing the peaks among them.

THIRTEEN

Step after step, I plugged up the steep snow slope. I shoved my ice axe into the soft snow to stabilise, then followed that with a kick-kick of each crampon for purchase against the slippery surface. The steady rhythm of my climbing gradually ate away at the altitude.

In the hundreds of metres of space beneath my boots, thick cloud swirled. It cloaked my companions in a haze the colour of dirty dishwater, visibility a paltry few metres. On either side of the narrowing snow gut we were ascending, dark walls of impassable rock angled in like closing curtains. The only sound was our heavy breathing, the occasional clatter of falling stones, and the hissing of snow as it sloughed from our steps.

I began to wonder if the route we'd committed to would work out. This is supposed to be a tramping pass, I told myself. This is supposed to be easy.

A voice fell through the gloom, echoing off the walls until

its origin was lost in the mist. A few minutes earlier, Jamie had clambered ahead up the gut, searching for a way over into Separation Stream. Now he was calling directions somewhere above us, ingested in the mass of cloud.

Jamie, Shelley, Troy Mattingley—Jamie's friend who had the rock climbing fall a few years earlier—and I were scratching around, high above Forbes Stream, trying to traverse from the Havelock River catchment into the Godley Valley. Initially, we had hoped to climb over Separation Col, across the glaciated eastern flank of Mount D'Archiac. Once over Separation Col, we were aiming to climb a new route on the western side of D'Archiac. But the thought of weaving through cavernous crevasses in a whiteout had us searching for an alternative route over Twilight Col instead.

This climb was to be one of many on our planned 200-kilometre alpine journey from Erewhon Station, inland of the Canterbury Plains, to the Otoko Valley north of Haast on the West Coast—just the kind of long, technical trip I had envisaged might be possible in New Zealand. The route involved traversing a portion of the Southern Alps and attempting a number of unclimbed mountain routes along the way. In all, it would take our team thirty-two days to complete.

We had already cycled 180 kilometres from Christchurch across the Canterbury Plains to Erewhon, and then picked our way up the braided valleys against a gusty northwesterly, before staring into blank infinity on Twilight Col. This was our first of many lessons on the trip: Backcountry travel would be dictated more by the weather than by our aspirations and endurance. But it was fine. This was what the four of us had intended. This was how we wanted to be challenged

'Nature's true wonders don't disclose themselves to day-trippers,' wrote the explorer Charlie Douglas. Considered by many to be the grandfather of transalpine travel in this country, 'Mr. Explorer Douglas' was renowned for completing difficult trips through some of our most remote valleys and passes during the 1800s. Over forty years, he explored and mapped hundreds of kilometres of west coast backcountry. While he didn't consider himself a climber, some of the mountainous terrain he covered was certainly more challenging than bush-whacking—sometimes for no better reason, noted John Pascoe in his biography Mr. Explorer Douglas, than 'to get a view'.

Douglas learned to travel and survive with meagre provisions. A bearded, compact, and shy man, he showed tenacity in atrocious weather and patience in trackless, fractured landscape, often travelling with only his dog—first Topsy and then Betsy-Jane—for company.

He was a keen observer of the environment and, in the days before freeze-dried food, supplemented his basic rations by hunting native birds and other wildlife. His tongue-in-cheek recipe for the flightless weka has become famous: Place one plucked and gutted weka into a pot of water. Add rocks and boil. After an hour, discard the weka and eat the rocks!

Hundreds were inspired to follow in the muddy footsteps of Douglas—including us. But transalpine trips can involve negotiating some of the most exposed topography in our mountains. Taking the least pleasant aspects of climbing and tramping and blending them into something else entirely, transalpine trips are the closest we get to backcountry expeditions in this landscape. Modern-day alpinists have benefited from more palatable food and better and lighter equipment, which has eased the burden a little. (For our team, technical equipment for attempting the unclimbed mountain routes added significantly to the weight in our packs.)

A life of ease was never on the agenda for Douglas. 'The impulse drove me out into the world, but the desire to then settle must have been omitted in my moral character, as here I am after thirty years wondering, crouched under a few yards of calico, with the rain pouring and the wind and thunder roaring among the mountains; a homeless, friendless vagabond, with a past that looks dreary and a future still more so,' he wrote on one wet exploration of the Waiatoto Valley. 'Still, I can't regret having followed such a life and I know that even if I and a thousand besides me perish miserably, the impulse which impels them to search the wild places of the Earth is good.'

I could relate to the words that Douglas wrote. For us, living in Christchurch after the earthquake had not been easy—our normal lives had become anything but. So much uncertainty remained around what would happen with broken homes and prolonged insurance claims. Heading into the hills on a journey like this was a much-needed escape on so many levels. It felt like an opportunity to reset the clock and start again.

Trident Tarns clung to the boulder-strewn northwestern slopes of Mount D'Archiac. Huge cracks in the earth illustrated how these mountains were being torn apart by rainfall, erosion and tectonic activity—like our lawn back in Christchurch but on a much larger scale. Nearby, deep canyons plunged hundreds of metres to the remnants of the Godley Glacier. It was an unnerving place to pitch our tents.

After crossing Twilight Col in the cloud and reaching our first food drop at Godley Hut, we ascended again. None of us had climbed in this remote pocket of the Southern Alps before, and we took turns orienting ourselves to the map.

The landscape felt alive with movement. Fat green grasshoppers threw themselves haphazardly from alpine grasses, and a disturbing large black spider terrified me for a moment while I filled my water bottle from a stream—much to the profound amusement of Shelley.

Swathes of dark clouds began to brew over the Main Divide at first light. Hoping to attempt D'Archiac's unclimbed northwest face, we scrambled across rocky outcrops, skirted more large cracks in the earth, and avoided the sprawling faces of rotting black argillite that looked as though they were about to disintegrate. The clouds kept churning, and by the time we traversed a hanging glacier to the base of the northwest face, it was threatening to rain. On day eight of the trip, our first climbing attempt was over before it started.

The weather didn't let up. Gale-force northwesterly winds, then low cloud and constant drizzle, accompanied us from the Godley across Armadillo Saddle into the Murchison Valley. It wasn't until lunchtime on day twelve that the sun finally broke free of its veil, hinting at another opportunity to climb a different mountain.

From our campsite on the edge of the moraine wall above Murchison Glacier, we clambered upwards towards the unclimbed west face of Mount Conrad. It was mid-afternoon by the time we had roped up to ascend Conrad's greywacke slabs. Sharing leads, we inched up steep corners and across broken ledges, searching for a route towards the summit ridge where no one had succeeded in the past.

Just after 7 p.m., we hoisted ourselves onto the summit ridge, tired but satisfied. It was our first summit of the trip. All of the planning and pack carrying had been worth it. Finally, we had been able to climb.

We hugged each other, then looked out over yet another dense system of cloud billowing to the west. All thought of success was quickly forgotten in the face of another approaching storm. By the time we returned to our tents, two hours later, the rain was about to start again.

Patchy weather continued the next day. We packed up our tents and climbed down a crumbly moraine wall onto the broken Murchison Glacier. We followed the melting ice of the Murchison, reaching its bulging terminal lake, before crossing the wide valley of the lower Tasman Glacier, and finally reaching Mount Cook Village.

It was time to regroup and replan the route for the weeks ahead. The worst storm of summer dumped half a metre of snow on the Mount Scissor slabs, our proposed pass from Mount Cook Village to the head of the Landsborough Valley, where our second supply drop lay waiting. A detour over Jamieson Saddle into the head of the Dobson Valley was inevitable, but the fresh snow would vex even that route, adding two days to a crossing that would ordinarily have taken a few hours.

Concerned about running out of food, we scavenged what we could from hut shelves in the Dobson and Hopkins Valleys. Self-doubt crept in. We—mostly Jamie and I—began to argue over the competing strategies of caution in the continuing bad weather, versus the desire we all shared to press on despite it. Our small group splintered into personal worlds of exhaustion. For the first time, I wondered if the four of us had the fortitude to complete the trip. The weather just wouldn't let up. Where had the summer disappeared to?

We struggled to Brodrick Hut, near the head of the North Huxley Valley, as another storm hit the mountains. Cold and soaking wet, we lit the fire and climbed into our sleeping bags. Outside, heavy rain and strong wind lashed the hut. The beech forest around our shelter creaked and groaned.

On day twenty-five, and down to our last meal, we finally crossed the Brodrick Pass and descended into the Landsborough Valley. We had something to smile about again. Our food drop was on the other side of the river, and the weather looked as though it might be settling.

The Landsborough was deep in Douglas' territory. He had spent many months exploring its reaches and wrote often of the birdlife he encountered there. While not beyond eating them, he enjoyed their company and had a particular soft spot for weka.

'Here is a bird full of good qualities and whose vices lean to virtue's side,' he wrote. 'Personal valour of a high order. An undying thirst for knowledge—unthinking people give it another name—which causes it to annex everything portable about a hut and carry off into the bush to study at leisure.'

It was not the weka but the inquisitive kea that kept us checking our gear. Though, like Douglas, we were treated to other boisterous birdlife, with sightings of long-tailed cuckoos, rock wrens, riflemen, robin, bellbirds, and feisty tui.

Our final alpine pass—the Upper Ōtoko—was also our most challenging. On day twenty-eight, we found ourselves contemplating a 70-degree rocky gut with the stability of kitty litter. There were no decent abseil anchors, which meant we couldn't use a rope. Back-tracking would have taken hours. I stared blankly at the others, took a deep breath, and slid into the gut after Jamie. We all managed to climb down the wall of fractured rock without too many pieces of it disintegrating in our hands, but it remains an experience firmly inscribed upon the list of 'Things I Never Want to Repeat'.

Two days later, Jamie and Shelley started up a new route on the north face of Mount Hooker. The length of the face and the amount of time it would take meant only two of us could climb. Also, one of the ropes was partially damaged from earlier rockfall, and no one was particularly keen to be solely tied in to that.

Troy and I followed the others up to the base of the face and watched as they climbed into the distance, becoming specks against its broad, rocky mass. We kept an eye on their progress, finally losing sight of them in a gully system. Even from our distant vantage point, the climbing appeared tenuous.

Later, Troy and I took turns scrambling up various boulders scattered around our camp to pass the time. Across the valley, a family of tahr chased each other across scree and snow with reckless abandon. The young frolicked so much that Troy and I stopped our own climbing to sit on the grass and watch them.

Upon dusk, Jamie and Shelley returned. They looked exhausted. 'I think that was the hardest and worst climbing I've ever done in the mountains,' said Jamie. 'No wonder no one has been able to get up the face before.'

Shelley dumped her pack by our tent and slumped onto the soft grass. 'I won't be recommending the route to anyone in a hurry,' she said.

They described long stretches of simul-climbing with only the twin ropes between them as there were no anchor points to belay from—one's life quite literally in the hands of the other as they inched their way up the wall. My jealousy from not being part of the climb dissipated a little at the thought of what they had experienced.

The following day, our second to last, we received the sort of welcome the West Coast is famous for. Rain fell in torrents, rock faces crashed with waterfalls, and the bush became heavy, humid, and slippery. We followed deer trails through thick forest down the Ōtoko Valley, camping at Stag Flat as the river flooded beside us. I was too wet and tired to worry about the weather. Even the sandflies lost their enthusiasm, hunkering down until the rain eased.

Our last day dawned fine and clear, though it couldn't displace an odd sense of melancholy. My desire for pizza, beer, and a shower was offset by a realisation that the simplicity of our existence over recent weeks was about to be shattered by an imminent return to the modern world.

Despite not being overseas, the trip had brought together prolonged exploration with technical mountaineering. It was the kind of trip that I had envisaged, and exactly what I needed.

It was also the kind of trip that reset the boundaries of what was possible in our mountains, highlighted why I climbed, and even perhaps helped define me as a person. It cemented the story of the land in my psyche, and made me appreciate who had gone before. And, it made me realise how lucky I was to have found a partner in Shelley, as well as such a strong bond with Jamie and a growing friendship with Troy. Climbing partnerships offer so much in terms of connection and trust. Just as you need to believe in yourself and then commit to the crux of a climb, the same can be said of having someone who believes in you and will commit to the climb with you.

The trip helped me to re-establish what was important in my life, especially when considering the experience of the Christchurch earthquakes, and then the near-miss while ice climbing with Shelley and Graham. It had given me time to contemplate: What experiences have the greatest worth? What might I do differently if I have another chance? Where do I want my life to lead in the future?

Whatever remained of our normal lives awaited our return. The uncertainty of a broken home in a broken city meant the idea of returning to it was less appealing than it might otherwise have been. A part of me even dreaded the return to Christchurch and the undoubted complications of post-earthquake life that lay before us. Remaining in the mountains seemed to be a much simpler and, in many ways, a much more attractive option.

As we walked the final few kilometres to Paringa and the Haast Highway, I thought of Douglas and his distaste of most things urban. In his final years, he became increasingly embittered towards 'easy living'. He preferred an uncluttered life in the wild, basic food, tobacco for his beloved pipe and, sometimes, good company. There was much to his pared-back philosophy towards living, as well as a lack of need for material possessions, that I could agree with.

'Fools think that knowledge can only be got from books and call me a fool for wasting my life in mountain solitudes,' wrote Douglas in late December 1902, deep in the Westland rainforest. 'But if in so doing I have found nothing new in thought or worth giving to the world, I have at least gathered glimmerings of truth as to how nature works, glimmerings which if they bear no fruit in this life, may in the next where darkness will be light.'

PART TWO

Light lifts like a ghost over hard country,
over a land falling away to nothing

FOURTEEN

See the young man standing on a dilapidated wooden lookout. He looks south towards the coast. Before him, a low-slung, grass-covered hill fades in and out of the cloud. The young man gazes past the hill, over dark, andesitic columns and walls of conglomerate rock that plunge into a space where the earth ends abruptly. He stares into that space. It is a space that only he can recognise.

Beyond is the ocean, slate-coloured and churned by winds that have blasted directly from the great southern ice.

Strange how the sea, especially in storm, reminds him of the mountains. The same definition of a boundary. The same unknown frontier. The same desire to discover. To let go.

Dirtied-white horses froth at the peaks of swells, as the waves slug away at coastal rock stacks waiting hundreds of metres beneath him. Even at the lookout, the salt spray films his face, damp and caustic. His chest constricts against the vortex of wind. He struggles to focus. This isn't love.

Driving out along the convoluted gravel road, he hadn't decided—or didn't know that he'd decided. But the sway of the grass back and forth, the sweep of the clouds with the wind, the sound of the surf's last throes, helped to convince him—reaching the cold abyss that lies within each of us.

The young man cups his hands and then rubs them together. The cold makes him feel better, more in the headspace he wants to be. The edginess is now a familiar feeling: a tightness in his neck and shoulders, a way that certain objects appear glass-clear while others fade toward insignificance.

'I just need time to myself, see where I'm at,' she'd explained a few weeks ago in a cafe boisterous with lunchtime excess.

He'd caught his breath then, holding back the sudden words he wanted to shout at her, to return the hurt. The voices at the next table formed a dull white noise that seemed to compress against him; her face blurring out of focus. He scraped back his chair and stood without replying. He'd already known.

A faint, narrow path leads down a spiny ridge on the far side of the lookout. Always, there's a way. Muddy and slippery, it jags steeply through scrub and rotten sheep droppings. He grabs a fistful of grass and slides over a short bluff. Here and there the track is undercut with erosion, and part has collapsed entirely. The air is heavy with spray and the sounds of the waves.

Through the vapour, a spire of rock breathes into view, a single, dark finger gesturing against the grey of the world.

Months earlier, they'd been at a pub in town, enjoying drunken banter with the locals. As always, she was articulate and engaging. He remained happy to sit and listen, watching the two of her—her reflection just as captivating against the *surface of the pub's dark windows. Her smile encouraged an old fisherman to join them in another round of drinks.*

'You climbing types would love it,' the fisherman had said, mostly to her. 'We call her The Maiden, but you can only see her properly from the water, standing there, still waiting for her lover after all these years.'

'How high?' she'd asked, leaning forward.

'What?' The old guy scratched at his scabby head, trying to work out the relevance of the question.

'How high is the stack? How big?'

'Buggered if I know. More than big enough to challenge your boy here, I'd warrant.'

'We should find it,' she'd said to him later, raising her hand, palm up above the table. 'Bet it's never been climbed.'

'For good reason, no doubt,' he'd replied. He spiralled his glass of beer. 'Probably a crumbly pile of choss, if it even exists.'

'Of course it bloody exists!'

He wonders now whether his pessimism was another factor. His negative way of making what he thought were the right decisions.

'Come climbing with us,' his friends had coaxed afterwards. 'It'll take your mind off things.'

But it hadn't. At the belay, he'd recalled climbing with her, how he'd poured so much energy into their relationship, working at what he thought she wanted. That wasted effort still haunts him. He thinks of her—tanned and strong, with long hair the colour of wet rock. As usual, he'd become infatuated with the physical, understanding nothing of what was important, what could last between them.

After she left, the texture of the rock, something he'd once relied upon, began to feel foreign. His fingers struggled to find *the right way to grip; his body always seemed slightly off balance.*

As a young boy, he'd imagined a kind of insulating layer in his mind, a shield. Whenever something troubled him at school, he could sit under a lone tree at the edge of the playing fields and the shield would descend over the branches like an invisible, protective dome. In past relationships, he'd been able to project an image behind that shield, a belief almost, of strength and confidence. But, this time, the image only made his insecurity more apparent, at least to him.

'Train harder, be stronger, climb better,' used to be his mantra. Yet it isn't physical ability he lacks.

'Don't worry, it's just a climber thing,' a friend had said, trying to console him. 'We become so focused, so intent on completing the task that some of us can't deal with failure, whatever it is. We say we can, but that's not the same.'

But now he feels as if his very fabric has ruptured, barely meshing what's left. There are no more crossroads in his mind, only a constricting corridor that surely must end. That needs to end.

He descends to a dip in the coast, a cove sheltered from the heaving sea and the wind's force. This is where she waits, he thinks, slipping into an old habit. To personify his climbs, he knows, is to place his own hopes and imperfections onto their curves and within their cracks. He doesn't care. Not any more.

Elongated, freestanding, and almost fragile in appearance, her edges rise nearly parallel towards the clouds. Beautiful. Enticing. Like an ill-timed voiceover, his thinking distances from his movement. With more purpose than he has felt for so long, he scrambles the last few metres over water-worn boulders, looks up at the conglomerate base and the toned andesite above. When they find my body, he thinks defiantly, they'll know what I was trying to do.

He starts tenderly, testing and weighting each hold before reaching for another. The stone feels chilled, sleek yet reassuring. But the surface of rocks can be deceitful. In a way, he has always known this. The elements have polished the minerals, dulled reds and greens within the fawn of the breccia. The wall is dark, slick with salt spray. Yet even though he's climbing in walking shoes, he starts to move efficiently. The commotion of the sea recedes. This feels different...better. Then his wet hands start slipping from the dimpled incuts. His shoes scrape against pocked slabs. He panics, but remembers: I just need to get high enough.

Seagulls squawk from their pedestals, and before long he joins them on a jut in the rock. Breathing heavily and shaking slightly, he laughs at having made it this far, almost ten metres off the ground already. Slowly, the breathing eases, and he looks up. A thin, sharp-edged crack points through the start of the andesite. Steep and damp, the crack looks too shallow and the faces on either side too smooth. Normally, this is where he'd baulk, even with a rope and climbing shoes. Now he reaches up and forces the fingers of one hand and then the other into the crack. He twists them sideways, and pulls.

I want this. I want them to see how good I can be.

The first moves are the hardest, his fingertips barely fitting and his shoes smearing across folds on the rock. Both feet slip off, and he's hanging by two knuckles. The seagulls seem to be holding their breath. Instead of cringing, he pulls in and reaches up with his other hand. So strong. So free. The crack widens, and now he can securely twist both hands and feet into it. He pauses.

For the first time, he looks down at the choppy surge of the sea, and then across at grey, broken cliffs along the main coast—the walls of a fortress. The cloud lifts for a while, allowing sunlight to sponge across their ramparts and catch in the wings of seabirds as they glide between the freestanding spire he is clinging to and the mainland.

The light allows him to judge how much height he has gained, and how far he has to go. He gently rests his head against a scoop of rock. This is ludicrous, he thinks. I can't even pick the right bloody way to end it! He struggles to move again. Why didn't I just jump? At least it would have been quick. But now I am here. Now, I have to do this.

His fingers run across the rock's surface, searching for any memories that its texture might inspire. Mental images begin to unveil, half-shrouded but enough to remind him of the essence of what really might have brought him here. Finally, he inches upward—the only thing he can do—following the crack that keeps broadening.

Armbar, shuffle, twist, thrutch. He focuses on the moves themselves, defining each position in his mind, and then the one after it, searching for a way back to his shield, for some means of forgetting where and who he is. Everything other than the right thing fades away to blurred peripheries.

The crack ends abruptly at a precarious crumbling ledge. Only a few metres away, a nightmarish jumble of stacked flakes separates him from the top of the pillar. He can see gannets circling overhead, rising and dipping with the wind, so close now.

It's too steep. I can't do it.

He squeezes his eyes shut and hugs the rock. Eventually, a measured breath comes.

She owes me this.

The first two holds disintegrate in his hands. He fights the suck of space, recovers, and starts hyperventilating. His ledge begins to disintegrate. He lunges for the most solid chunk of rock he can see, wrapping both hands around it as the last of the ledge peels away, crumbling and falling, slowly at first, then accelerating, bouncing once, twice, before slapping into the sea.

NnnggggFFaaarrrrkkk! The gannets scatter before his sudden arrival at the top of the pillar. He stays on his knees for a time, pulling deep breaths into his lungs and pushing his hands into the soil and bird shit. Slowly, he stands and then yells into the clouds, partially for help but mostly an elemental release. His voice echoes between the cliffs. He shuffles cautiously to the edge and peers over, wondering for a moment but then shaking his head.

Shadows stretch across the land. He starts shivering, and curls with his hands between his legs. The wind has eased. The sea begins to calm. The last of the light flickers across smoothing ocean swells, broken mirrors reflecting back towards him. He keeps his eyes open. He prays for the slow, cold draw toward the dark not to end.

At nightfall, the temperature drops, holding him conscious for a time. He talks to himself, his chattering teeth unable to form the words.

He hopes someone might come in the morning. He thinks he has the right to hope because, if nothing else, she has finally accepted him. Of course, he dreams of her again, languid, floating, the two of them climbing as a team should. Then, when he looks back, he doesn't see her anymore. There is simply more rock, another climb.

He wakes quickly, as if someone has kicked him. The inevitability of his situation begins to sink in, and he hopes he won't become delirious in the end. Perhaps, believing he is warm, he might take off his clothes. 'Naked man found stranded on top of pillar'—*now that would make for a story!*

He lies there, shivering in the frigid dark, wondering whether this, any of this, is worth it. Not long before the cold finally takes him, he realises the worth of a thing doesn't really come in to it. Not now anyway. Not anymore.

Loss, confusion, and regret drove me to write the words above. To need to write them. To try to contain the helplessness that was threatening to overwhelm me. To make sense of how I felt even though I realised there was likely no sense to be found. To find hope.

Shock and then grief are not particularly enlightening states of mind to have to deal with, but they are necessary. If old age and pessimism has taught me anything, it's that tackling something head-on rather than beating around the bush is a better place to start if I want to reach a conclusion. And, any way that I can manufacture hope in my own mind, as well as supporting others, is worth a go.

If I'm being honest, it was probably anger that I felt the most. I was struggling to find the right way to express myself—a writer and a climber in risk of losing both of his crafts. My anger was not directed towards anyone in particular, just life. I was angry that life did this. That life can *do* this. That life is this and, sometimes, nothing more. Even now, there are still times that I get close to wanting no part of it, especially if always being prepared to face the unexpected is the only way to live. Doing so creates a certain hardness to all of my thoughts.

Yes, I'd been here before. But that knowledge didn't make it any easier. Perhaps the knowing made it worse. Hopefully, my love for family and friends, and for the mountains and of climbing them, would help in the process, in understanding the what and the why, and then using that to instigate the start of healing. Again! In the past, I'd always managed to account for a decision—my decision—eventually.

But, for the time being, I struggled to make sense. The whys and why nots just felt like superficial, self-justifying bullshit. My misdirected anger only added to my confusion, which, in turn, made me more angry. Let me climb into infinity, curl up in that cold, dark space where no one can find me, and hope to forget.

FIFTEEN

Mahe was born on the last day of January in the year 2013. Of course, Jamie and Jess doted on him. Jamie was so excited about the challenges that fatherhood would bring. He had a glint in his eyes that I had seen many times before. It was the same glint he would get climbing or surfing or making kickass pizza and bread for his family and friends—doing things that gave him a sense of purpose, that made him feel alive.

It was certainly a time for change. A few months before Mahe's birth, Shelley and I made the difficult decision to move away from our home and close friends in Christchurch. The drudgery of post-earthquake life had become too much. Our house needed to be demolished, and we weren't keen to invest the insurance payout in more property in Christchurch, especially given all of the ongoing drama and uncertainty around land instability and new building code requirements.

So, we shifted back to Dunedin. We bought a house

on the coast just north of the city, right next to the sea and within walking distance of the Silver Peaks. Step by step, we built normality back into our lives. We kept heading into the mountains, meeting Jamie when he was free and keen to climb, and also managing to catch up with Marty the few times he was back in New Zealand between his many overseas expeditions.

Around the same period, Jamie said to me that he wanted to step away from what he saw as some of our riskier mountaineering objectives. He wanted less explorative trips, replacing them with technical routes that were easier to access—routes that he reckoned could be 'safer' than what we had been attempting.

'I've got responsibilities now,' he said. 'I need to be around for Mahe.'

Of course, I understood. Although it meant we would be climbing less together in the future, a part of me realised that Jamie and I had probably been starting to head in different directions with our climbing. Jamie wanted to try harder technical objectives with stronger climbers, while I remained happy exploring the less obvious corners of our environment, to find lines of weakness in the terrain that inspired me. Our climbing partnership was waning.

I knew that Jamie had been working towards a new way of thinking with his climbing, something he later called 'the lines of most resistance'. Reflecting on a recent trip, where he climbed difficult new routes with another talented alpinist Jono Clark, Jamie wrote afterwards that 'it wasn't the technical difficulties per se that stuck in my mind, but more so the attitude we took when we chose our lines and then climbed them. The way we did this opened my eyes to a whole new dimension. I would no longer be blinkered by lines of weakness when I sought new ways to climb mountains. Instead, I sought lines of most resistance'.

Jamie's approach to mountaineering was developing—maturing, perhaps—and that was fine by me. A part of me was even relieved at his change in direction. It meant that I wouldn't have to train so hard to keep my fitness level as high. I also wouldn't feel as pressured to climb close to or beyond my limit, and my conservative decision-making wouldn't be challenged so often or perceived as a potential barrier to Jamie's climbing progression. I could focus on the parts of mountaineering that appealed to me. I could even try to extend my experience in the Greater Ranges overseas.

Yes, 2013 felt like a year of change. But change meant opportunity. All of us had goals in the mountains and plans on how to reach those goals. But goals and plans, like dreams, are sometimes nothing more.

It was May 2013. I was glued to my computer, waiting for news about a good friend who was battling to stay alive on a mountain in Nepal. Scott Blackford-Scheele was part of a New Zealand team attempting the previously unclimbed Anidesha Chuli (6815m) near Jannu, in eastern Nepal. This was White Wave, the same mountain I had seen in the photos in Graeme Dingle's book *Wall of Shadows* all those years earlier. Initially, Shelley and I were meant to be involved in Scott's expedition. But, we had to withdraw due to the ongoing financial constraints from the damage to our home and section in the Christchurch earthquakes, and then buying new property in

Dunedin.

Scott took a bad fall during a summit push on Anidesha Chuli with Ben Dare. Ben managed to lower Scott back down to their high camp, and they were later joined by other team members Rob Frost and Andrei van Dusschoten who had climbed through the night to reach them.

With Scott suffering from a serious head wound as well as other injuries, he and Ben were then airlifted in a challenging high altitude helicopter rescue and flown to a hospital in Kathmandu. The story made national news in New Zealand, and Ben was rightly hailed as a hero for getting his climbing partner back to safety. They did everything they could when things started to go awry, and to me, this was the epitome of great teamwork.

While I anxiously waited for an update on Scott's condition, reports started filtering through the media of a major altercation on Everest. Apparently, three European climbers were involved in an argument with a team of Nepalese Sherpa on the Lhotse Face of Everest. And then they were assaulted by a much larger group of Sherpa once everyone had returned down to Camp 2.

I knew that a number of friends, including Marty, were working and climbing on Everest that season. I followed the unfolding story with growing concern. While much of the mainstream and social media coverage focussed on what could only be described as a frenzy of allegations and denials, I tried to filter through the supposition and opinions to work out what actually happened and why.

The three westerners involved were high profile, sponsored climbers Ueli Steck from Switzerland and Simone Moro from Italy, along with Briton Jon Griffith. They had been soloing the steep snow/ice slope between Camp 2 and 3, at around 7000 metres. At the same time, a team of Sherpa had been laying fixed lines for the contingent of commercial guiding companies, and for the large number of clients who paid them—and needed their assistance—to have any chance of reaching the summit.

As the trio crossed over the ropes on the way to their tent at Camp 3, apparently a disagreement or shouting match broke out. The Sherpa later claimed that one of them had been hit by ice that was dislodged by the westerners, an allegation denied by the three climbers.

When Steck, Moro, and Griffith returned to Camp 2, a much larger group of Sherpa (estimates are between 50–100) attacked them, punching and kicking them and throwing rocks. Other foreign climbers—including Marty—intervened (as did some Sherpa), trying to calm the situation for long enough so that the three could escape through the Khumbu icefall, and to Base Camp further down the mountain.

This sounds like sheer madness on the slopes of the world's highest mountain. It's hard enough trying to stay safe in such an extreme alpine environment without adding physical confrontation to the risk. The contrast between people threatening each other on Everest and my mates battling to stay alive on Anidesha Chuli couldn't have been greater.

How can we make sense of this serious, and by all accounts near-death, altercation? The three climbers involved reported on their very scary experience—all claiming innocence of doing anything wrong. Ueli Steck believed he would have been killed if others, including Marty, hadn't intervened. Meanwhile, some westerners took the Sherpa's side to the story, stating that the three climbers had been arrogant and disrespectful towards them. And, then, plenty of other climbers and non-climbers offered comments and viewpoints over why this might have occurred, who had been slighted, and the perceived implications of the incident.

I had contact with some of my friends who were there, but they tried to keep their heads down in the aftermath. As part of various commercial guiding teams, they needed to keep working with the Sherpa and working for their clients.

Ed Hillary would likely be rolling in his grave. He was never a fan of Everest being guided, and would no doubt be frowning those bushy eyebrows of his at how cumbersome the whole business had become. One busy day on Everest recently saw more than two hundred people summit. The guiding companies charge large sums—upwards of $50,000 NZ—for an attempt on the mountain the Nepalese call Chomolongma. But the fact remains, people want to climb it, and they are willing to pay whatever the cost.

New Zealanders have been involved in guiding Everest for several years, and 2013 was no exception. Along with Marty, Lydia Bradey (the first woman and first New Zealander to summit Everest without supplementary oxygen) was hoping to reach the top for the third time while guiding for Adventure Consultants, while Mike Roberts was going for his seventh successful ascent, and Dean Staples and Mark Woodward were trying for their ninth.

Intrinsic to this commercial operation are the Sherpa. Until the early 1950s, no high Himalayan peak in Nepal had ever been climbed. But as an insatiable desire for the high summits developed—especially for Everest—the Sherpa were seen and used as local labour by the visiting climbers. Some would say this relationship developed into a more evenly footed relationship over time, but others would disagree. At any rate, the inexplicable passion among a small, wealthy western elite for exploring the mountains of the Sherpa homeland, together with the Sherpa's ability to cope with the altitude, gave these people a chance to escape their more difficult subsistence living, herding yaks or carrying loads for traders.

For Sherpa and foreign guides, the job of establishing and fixing a route up Everest could be described as a tense working situation. They toil long hours beside each other. The stakes are high. They need to establish a safe route over difficult, dangerous terrain for hundreds of climbers and guided clients. Arguments happen, as they do in most workplaces—among the westerners, among Sherpa, and occasionally between Sherpa and westerners.

According to Adventure Consultants guiding company boss Guy Cotter, there had been altercations between western teams and the Sherpa before, but none as public as the one in 2013. 'The climbing season on Everest, by nature, is a time of high stress where everybody has a lot at stake,' he said. 'People of different nationalities are forced to work together in pressure-cooker situations and this brings out the best and the worst in them.'

It would be easy to point the finger at the commercialisation of Everest and blame the big guiding companies for bringing this conflict into the local communities. But, if you take the mountain away, this type of conflict also exists in other tourism activities where tourists from developed nations recreate in less developed countries. Another example I can think of—and have experienced—is surfing in Bali, Indonesia. In recent years, the number of altercations has greatly increased over waves—over what is, essentially, a limited resource. Whether it be resentment, jealousy, competition, greed, or a lack of cultural understanding, differing factors can motivate individuals or groups into anger and violence.

Despite the tensions and potential conflicts, climbing Everest is big money for the guiding companies, the Sherpa, and the Nepalese Government. After the 2013 bust-up, the government moved quickly to quell any ongoing problems. Meetings were organised, agreements signed, and handshakes offered. Pledges were made to consider everyone's position, while at the same time trying to move on from the unsavoury incident as discreetly as possible.

So, would an event like this change things on Everest? Probably not, according to Cotter. 'Even though it's been almost universally banned as a subject that can be discussed, different nationalities react differently to different challenges and this situation is a prime example,' he said. 'At the end of the day, it proves once again that a bit of respect goes a long way when dealing with others and we should be even more cognisant of this in situations with other cultures, especially in their own homeland.'

I'll leave the final words to my friend Marty, who blogged this after the incident: 'No matter what is talked about in the media, this powerful place will always be filled with a peaceful, inner solace for every human being to experience. It calls many people to its base, from trekkers to fly by sight-seers to us mountaineers. It has since 1921 from the Tibetan side with Mallory and from 1952, with the Swiss from the Nepalese side. This is Chomolongma, the goddess mother of this earth. There is a total respect toward these mountains surrounding us every day. Us climbers are in harmony with what we are called to do and have great respect for the Sherpa climbers. This relationship will always be worked on and will always be improved with a non-ego approach and with total respect from both sides. On this mountain, we all need to work together to make it a safe and successful climb for everyone every year.'

The following month, a far greater tragedy occurred in the mountains. What later became known as the 'Nanga Parbat Massacre' took place in Pakistan on June 22. Reports were that around sixteen militants—from a village near Chilas where I had stayed on my expedition with Pat a few years earlier—stormed the mountain's Base Camp. There, they shot and killed ten foreign climbers and one local tourist guide.

The climbers killed were from various countries, including Ukraine, China, Slovakia, Lithuania, and Nepal. One Chinese citizen managed to evade the assailants by running and hiding in the surrounding countryside. A Latvian member of the group, who happened to be away from the camp during the attack, also escaped the massacre.

Thinking about my own travel through this region, I was shocked to find out about it. This shooting was the first time an attack on mountaineers had occurred in the Gilgit-Baltistan region of Pakistan, somewhere which, compared to other areas in the country, had been generally considered free from terrorism. I wondered how it would affect the perception of Pakistan and the Pakistani people, and again slant western perceptions against them and their culture. It also helped put the incident on Everest into perspective.

SIXTEEN

The altercation on Everest, and then the mass killing on Nanga Parbat, made me all the more aware of the plans we were forming for our own upcoming expedition. While our trip was still a year out, the planning didn't feel too hectic. But then it was only eight months. There were still many different aspects to coordinate. The training intensified. Gear piled up until the spare room in our Dunedin house started to look like a bomb site. Maps and photos were studied endlessly. Emails were sent back and forth with the overseas logistics company about every contingency that we could come up with. And then, before we realised it, it was time to buy the flight tickets. The full commitment, or a final chance to bail.

After the previous New Zealand expedition had failed—the trip that Scott needed rescuing on—Shelley and I decided to attempt Anidesha Chuli ourselves. But, due to my trip to Pakistan and the challenges experienced, I was a bit dubious about committing to another expedition. I wasn't concerned about the risk of a terrorist attack in Nepal. But, I had never attempted a mountain the height of Anidesha Chuli before, and I wondered how my body would cope with the increase in altitude.

Doubts clouded my mind, like always, but I applied my positive power of negative thinking. And this time I would be climbing with Shelley and another good friend, John Price—partners I could depend on and who could depend on me.

The expedition also seemed an ideal opportunity to utilise the climbing experiences I had with Jamie and the knowledge I had gathered from Marty. It was something that would require all of my skills. No doubt it would test me. My journey through life—how far I had progressed—was again being measured by mountains.

As Shelley and John and I prepared for our new challenge, I knew that Marty and his son Denali were already on their own expedition, trying to climb K2. While Everest, at 8849 metres as the world's highest mountain, is generally acknowledged in non-climbing circles—along with Aoraki / Mount Cook, it's usually the only mountain non-climbers ask whether I've climbed it or must want to climb it—few would have heard of the second-highest mountain, K2.

Despite the notorious and unpredictable Khumbu Icefall access to the most popular south side of Everest in Nepal, K2 in Pakistan is considered much more difficult and dangerous to ascend. K2 is a climber's mountain. It is also referred to as a savage mountain, a killer mountain. Approximately one person is killed trying to climb it for every four who manage to reach its summit at 8611 metres.

Perhaps K2's reputation is part of the allure. The most

commonly attempted and climbed route is the Abruzzi Spur, the southeast ridge of the peak. Rising like an awkward-looking knuckle above Advanced Base Camp (at 5400 metres), the start of the route involves negotiating a series of convoluted rock ribs and snow/ice fields, including surmounting two famous rock features, House's Chimnney and the Black Pyramid. Above this, the ridge broadens in a snow slope leading towards an area known as the Shoulder, and then it pinches again at the Bottleneck before the final push to the summit.

Even though the Abruzzi Spur is the route most commonly attempted on K2, it is still steep, exposed, committing, and dangerous.

Marty made his first attempt on K2 via the Abruzzi back in 1992, the year after his daughter, Sequoia, was born. Marty got within 200 metres of the summit before being forced to turn around due to severe wind. Although unsuccessful, he left the mountain determined to again make that exposed traverse above the 'Bottleneck', beyond the ever-present threat of the hanging seracs, and then up the final, steep snow slope to the highest point in Pakistan.

Marty made a second attempt in 2000, but once again failed to reach the top because of adverse conditions that season.

'I've climbed a lot of the world's biggest mountains, but K2 is the one I respect the most,' he once said. 'I'm just called to it all the time.'

Denali, increasingly sharing his father's love for the higher mountains and the extended challenge of trying to climb them, was asked by Marty to join him for his third attempt on K2, in 2013.

It was on July 25 when Marty, Denali, and their Australian

climbing partner, Chris Warner, ascended from Base Camp directly to Camp 2 at 6700 metres on the Abruzzi. One of seven teams on the southeast ridge that season, the three made good time up the spur, finding a site amongst the other climbers at Camp 2 to level a platform in the snow that was wide enough to fit their tent. As evening approached, they prepared dinner and discussed what conditions might be like higher on the mountain.

Chris explained afterwards that everyone seemed healthy and had coped well with the quick ascent up to Camp 2. 'We all felt strong,' he said.

As a warm-up for K2, they had already climbed another mountain nearby, Broad Peak. At 8047 metres, it is the world's twelfth highest summit and an ideal acclimatisation for the higher and more difficult K2.

The three teammates were well-rested after Broad Peak. And they were keen to try for the summit of K2 in alpine style (meaning a single push without using pre-established camps). This was not a typical way of attempting a mountain as high or challenging as K2, but the method was well within their ability. Marty had used this technique to great success on some of his other 8000 metre climbs.

Later in the evening, other climbers passed Marty, Denali, and Chris' tent with reports that a team of Sherpa had failed to break trail through the snow up to Camp 3, at 7200 metres. The Sherpa had been trying to reach and restock the site. Eventually, the Sherpa also returned to Camp 2, reporting unstable, 'sluffing' snow higher on the mountain, and having to wade waist to chest deep through it to make any progress.

Hearing about such poor conditions further up the Abruzzi, most of the twenty or so climbers and other Sherpa recovering at Camp 2 decided to descend immediately to Base

Camp. Given what had been discovered above, there seemed little point in remaining at a higher altitude, especially given that the weather opportunity for settled climbing conditions over the next few days was predicted to be small. It would be much easier to conserve their energy down at Base Camp. Discussions continued among those who stayed overnight at Camp 2 about whether to go up, remain where they were, or also descend back to Base Camp the following morning.

Marty, Denali, and Chris talked about what to do. 'We had only been on the mountain a day,' Chris reported afterwards. So far on the Abruzzi, they had found little new snow on the way up to Camp 2, but understood that conditions could be variable across the peak depending on the aspect and altitude of the slope they were ascending.

Rather than just relying on the reports of others, the three talked about judging the conditions further up the mountain for themselves. According to Chris, they agreed on at least 'checking it out' the following day.

Marty, Denali, and Chris slept well that night, or about as well as anyone can crammed together in a small tent at such a high altitude. Gentle but consistent snowfall continued to fall through the night, with Chris remembering about fifteen centimetres of new snow underfoot around their tent the next morning.

It was then that Chris changed his mind about continuing with the climb. As they were making tea for breakfast, he told Marty and Denali that he now wanted to descend like the other teams were doing. To continue, he said afterwards, 'didn't seem to add up in my head as a good decision in regards to safety or our progress to the summit. I really thought we would just go up and come down possibly without making Camp 3, and what was the point of that?'

Chris didn't think they could make the summit given the reported snow conditions higher, especially now that other climbers had descended or were planning to go down that morning. They would be the only team remaining on the upper mountain, which meant they would have to do all of the trail breaking through new snow themselves—a huge effort at such an altitude.

'We could always wait and come back up again,' Chris said. 'But I knew Marty was on a certain path upwards and (might) think of me as quitting.'

When Chris stated his intention to descend, Marty accepted his decision without comment.

It was around 8:00 or 9:00 a.m., and no one seemed in a great rush to do anything. Marty, Chris, and Denali conversed with other climbers as they prepared to leave camp. Then Chris started to pack his own gear, getting ready to follow everyone else down. Marty and Denali would be the only ones who remained at Camp 2.

'The more people went down, the more [Marty] wanted to go up,' Chris reported later. 'We rearranged the gear, as they were now two. We left each other in good spirits, and I said I would stay in contact over the radio. I swallowed my ego and descended from Camp 2, feeling that I had blown my summit chance as these two were heading to the top.'

That night, after safely descending the lower Abruzzi and reaching Base Camp, Chris tried to make contact with the Kiwis during the scheduled 6:00 p.m. call. There was no reply, but he continued to try to reach them for about an hour afterwards.

Finally, Marty responded. He stated that the two of them

had safely reached Camp 3. They would make a decision whether to continue further up the mountain in the morning, and would relay this back to Chris at the scheduled 8:00 a.m. radio call.

However, the next day, none of the calls to the Schmidts were answered. Then another night passed. The following morning, with still no contact from Marty or Denali, two Sherpa made a brave decision to climb back up the Abruzzi to try to see what had happened.

Reaching the site of Camp 3, it was obvious a large avalanche had released from above and hit the area. The Sherpa discovered scattered ice axes and other gear, but they couldn't find any sign of either Marty or Denali. The whole campsite had been obliterated.

SEVENTEEN

My friend Kester Brown sent me an email about the avalanche at Camp 3 two days after it had happened. By that stage, Marty and Denali were still missing, and they were presumed dead.

This wasn't the first time I had been forced to read about the death of a friend in the mountains, but it still felt like a knife being jammed between my shoulder blades. Emotions and memories threatened to overwhelm me as I re-read the short report of their loss. I closed my eyes. I focussed on taking deep breaths, one after the other, in through my nose and out through my mouth. Just trying to relax. To let the feelings wash over me. Then I read Kester's email for the third time, as if the words or the implications of the words could somehow change if I kept reading and willed them to enough.

Despite the initial shock, I found myself trying to slip into justification mode. Yes, I understood the added dangers of attempting to climb a mountain like K2—as did Marty—and I used this justification as some type of ledger to balance against his and Denali's deaths.

Over the following days, I chose to focus on the positive influence that Marty had on my life and no doubt on the lives of many others who'd known and loved him. He and Denali were doing something that they valued and loved, and they were well aware of the risks involved.

Reflecting on this now, I think a main part of me trying to justify things so promptly was because of our own upcoming expedition to Anidesha Chuli. I needed to find a way in my mind to accept that outcomes like this can happen in the mountains and to decide that it was still okay for us to go. So, instead of dealing with the loss, I chose to focus on what Marty had achieved in the mountains, as well as the good he had done in his life.

In a climbing community that had its share of larger-than-life characters, Marty stood taller than most. It was so many years earlier when I first met him. Since then, our paths had crossed a number of times, including during the terrible challenges of the Christchurch earthquakes. We had our stories of near misses, and we shared them over coffee in his broken kitchen, and wine in our sharply-leaning lounge. Both of us listened to the other and then offered support or advice where we could.

At a potluck dinner at our house, Marty accidentally threw a glass of red wine across the table and over half the dinner guests while retelling another of his expansive adventures. Some at the table stared wide-eyed, not knowing what to do or how to respond. The rest of us burst into laughter: that was classic Marty. I was reminded yet again of his intense enthusiasm for pretty much every aspect of life. I felt incredibly privileged to consider him as both a climbing mentor and a friend.

Thinking of Marty now makes me want to strive to be a better person. To step forward more often. To be less afraid or, if I am afraid, to still be able to act despite having that knowledge. I imagine he would want me to believe in myself more than I tend to do, and not to let so many self-doubts consume my motivation and ability. He would want me to keep testing and increasing my limits, to prepare better, and to not give up so easily. *Always strive. Never stop learning. Never be satisfied.*

Ahh, Marty, the world is a far lesser place without your energy and enthusiasm and drive to squeeze every fulfilling drop out of what life might offer.

When things like this happen, naturally they make that analytical part of my mind wonder again if the cost of mountaineering is too high. In the aftermath of loss, I couldn't help but question my own desire again. But part of me also wondered why I needed to justify my decisions. Why couldn't I make choices within the freedom of living, without justification or reasoning? Simply live in the act and the moment.

But then I recognised the selfishness of such thinking. Marty and Denali's deaths were yet another reminder of what can go wrong in the mountains, to go with the losses of other friends and acquaintances before them. The reminder was especially poignant given the overseas expedition Shelley, John, and I were well into planning. It was at the stage where we needed to book and pay for flights. Either we committed to the trip or we didn't.

Even though I could imagine Marty chastising me for thinking such a thing, a part of me felt it would have been more respectful not to go. Maybe we should just leave it for a season or two. Perhaps, even a year would be enough to let the dust settle over the death of yet another friend to the mountains.

Then, I caught up with Jamie. After also hearing the news, and knowing how close I was to Marty, he called to see how I was doing. We talked about the tragedy that unfolded on K2, and how it made us feel about our own climbing ambitions. I told my friend that I was considering cancelling our Nepal expedition. When I tried to weigh up the pros and cons, and especially given the serious accident that Scott had experienced on Anidehsa Chuli the previous season, it all just seemed too much. Maybe I was better off choosing a less challenging mountain, or one that was of a lower altitude than Anidesha Chuli

Jamie was quick to try and convince me that I'd regret any decision not to go. It was just another expedition, he said, just like all of the other expeditions I had previously been on, both successful and unsuccessful.

'Be careful,' he added. 'Make safe decisions. You're good at that, Paul. It's a strength of your climbing.'

Jamie seemed so certain of his judgement that I didn't think, or perhaps have the energy, to argue anymore. Instead, our conversation moved on to what snow and ice conditions might be like on the Remarkables Mountain Range, which overlooks Queenstown. There was a climbing festival happening there in about a week, and Jamie was heading down a few days before me. We made tentative plans to catch up there again, and hopefully get to climb one of the ice and mixed routes together if we found the time.

Jamie told me that he was looking forward to Jess and Mahe also travelling down with him. They would be able to enjoy the sights of Queenstown as he climbed during the day, and then they could all be together in the evening. For him, it was the best of both worlds.

It was still dark on Monday morning, August 12, when Jamie and his climbing partner Steve Fortune drove up the road to the carpark at the base of the Remarkables Ski Field. The road and ski field are the main access for climbing on Single Cone and Double Cone. Jamie had left the holiday house, where he was staying with Jess and Mahe, and then texted her at around 6:30 a.m. to let her know where he was on the mountain.

There had been a storm earlier in the week, and some new windblown snow had accumulated across various slopes. But, it was not enough for Jamie or Steve to be concerned about unsafe conditions on the mountain.

The two climbers quickly ascended the groomed trails on the ski field, well before any skiers or snowboarders had arrived. Leaving the ski field boundary, they then traversed an area known by climbers as the Queen's Drive—in summer a broad scree shelf, and in winter a gradually-angled but exposed ramp of snow. Beyond that, a series of isolated, snow-filled gullies led to their planned climbing route for the day on the western side of the Remarkables Range.

As they traversed the slopes west of Single and Double Cone, Jamie and Steve set off and were caught in a small, localised avalanche in one of the snow gullies. Steve managed to use his ice axe to stop himself from sliding too far in the loose snow, but Jamie's untethered axe was knocked from his grasp. His slip gathered momentum. Unable to self-arrest, he quickly fell from Steve's sight.

The first moment I realised something had happened was when another climber—someone I knew who was also in Queenstown—posted on social media that they were safe. I sent a short text to Jamie. I can't remember exactly what I typed, probably something like: 'What's up? Has something happened?' I sat and waited for his reply. There were the smallest of anxious voices in my mind, but I stilled them. *It's Jamie! He's the strongest climber I know.*

Shelley was standing beside me when the phone rang a few minutes later. I recognised the caller: it was Alistair Walker, another good friend and climber from Otago. Al had many contacts in the wider climbing community.

'Hi, Paul,' he said, and straightaway I knew from his tone that what he was about to tell me wasn't something I wanted to hear. I took a deep breath to calm my suddenly racing mind. I turned and looked towards Shelley as I listened to Al's quiet, measured voice on the other end of the phone.

'Look,' my friend continued. 'I'm sorry but I've got some bad news. There's no easy way to say this...'

I probably didn't need to hear the rest of Al's words. In my heart, I already knew what he was about to say.

'Okay, thanks, Al,' I finally replied. 'Thanks for letting me know so soon. I appreciate you making the call.'

Over the years, mountaineering has taught me how to keep operating when something goes horribly wrong. I listened to Al's words. I went to that dark, quiet place in my mind where I didn't want to be found. Where I imagined I could be safe. *Keep moving. Keep making decisions. Keep breathing.*

Shelley was still looking at me. I swallowed to get my mouth to work. To reform the words. Words are just words, after all.

After a time, I found enough courage to call Jess. I searched for her number in my contacts. I had no idea what to say.

'Everything that ever was, and ever will be, is here right now in this moment. Do not seek to control it, but instead feel it and trust in it. This is the rhythm of life. When you entrust yourself to this rhythm there is no right or wrong, only the spontaneity of pure being. This way of being is not an end in itself, but a way that does not hinder the harmony or purpose of life.'

Jamie wrote these words. At his funeral service, before a sea of light-shrouded, grieving faces—of Jess, and Jamie's parents and his brother, and his many friends, climbers and otherwise—I spoke of how much I treasured my relationship with him. I explained how he'd inspired me to strive for things even if I didn't think I'd be able to reach them. Jamie always liked to challenge me, not just my physical ability, but also my ideas and my way of thinking—especially if they differed from his. Along with our shared climbing memories, it was one of the things I valued most about our friendship.

I can see him now, sitting across from me with a craft beer in his hand. No doubt, he'd be prodding me to find something positive from the experience.

'Come on, Paul,' he'd say with a cheeky grin—just like he did whenever I was trying to follow a challenging section of a route that he had breezed up. 'All that thinking and writing you do. What's your intuition on this? Give us some insight.'

I don't know that I have any particularly well-considered insight, but maybe an observation: when we lose someone close, suddenly like this, at some stage in the grieving process we come to realise what it was about them that we valued so highly. Yet, we don't always recognise this so much, or openly express it, when they're still alive. It takes the loss of it to fully understand the worth of a thing.

I never told Jamie how much I appreciated his company and valued his friendship, how much I cared for his views— even though they occasionally caused conflict between us. I never told him how much I admired his attitude to life, his fierce love for his family, and his loyalty to friends. We had some pretty snuggly, sleepless nights together on bleak, windswept mountainsides, but that's not the same as saying the words to him, is it?

Well, maybe in a way, it is. Maybe, as Jamie often illustrated to me, it is a case that actions are or can be stronger than words as a means towards understanding. Sometimes it is better not to think so much. Sometimes it is enough to believe and to act.

By choosing to climb together, the time we shared in the mountains was, in part, an attempt to gain perspective—not just of ourselves but also how we fitted into the scheme of things. How we judged. How we adapted. How we needed to keep reassessing what we valued. How we craved challenge and adventure, and the simplicity that brought to our lives. And how we treasured sharing our goals.

Jamie's death affected many people, not just his family and close climbing friends. His was a positive influence on the wider climbing community, and on many others not involved with climbing. Like Marty, he tried to support those who he thought needed help with some aspect of their lives.

While many of us may recognise when others need help, often we become so tangled in our own issues that we lack the energy to extend a much-needed hand. Sometimes even small acts of kindness make all the difference. I try to remind myself of this as often as I can.

An example of Jamie's attitude towards helping others was immediately after the Christchurch earthquake. For many of our non-climbing friends, things like preparing basic meals on a gas cooker in an otherwise non-functioning kitchen or digging a hole in the back yard for rather exposed ablutions, seemed like a big and, at times, stressful deal. To us outdoorsy types, it was almost normal. It didn't feel too dissimilar to another trip in the mountains. We knew what needed to be done, so we just hunkered down and got on with it.

Jamie reached out to many of his neighbours and friends who were in need. His actions were an example for the rest of us to follow. He encouraged us to help those that we could, to find satisfaction in even the smallest things, and to share humour through what might otherwise have been, for some, impossibly dark times.

EIGHTEEN

Night's veil rose from the sea like a parting of the fog. There was a decent north swell rolling towards shore, the remnants of Cyclone Lucy, which had given the country a good pounding earlier in the week. Waves radiated towards land, the ocean's pulse, which was also my lifeblood on many a glass-sculpted, windless day such as what the coming dawn was about to reveal.

I'd risen early, not just for the promise of surf, but because I hadn't been able to sleep again. Back home, down the narrow lick of wet sand that my footprints would disappear from with the next tide, a pile of bags was packed. Each item within them had been scrutinised, as if it alone might hold the key to my safety and that of my wife and climbing partner. The high summits of the Himalaya called to me, but it was with an edgy ear that I heeded that call.

When I was younger, I figured I could control much of my

life. But, really, the randomness of it seemed to be the deciding factor in most things. All I wanted from the mountains was to have adventures and fun with my friends, and to be able to make good, safe decisions. But these felt like they counted for nothing when I was faced with the reality of having someone important taken from me.

My desire had vanished, my self-belief shredded. I needed to find a way to convince myself that I was making the right call. *We aren't diving headlong into disaster. We've prepared well and we will make the best decisions possible during every stage of the expedition.*

So I revisited Jamie's writing, thinking about our many trips together and our shared experiences. I was searching for a perspective, or a reasoning, that might help with my own indecision.

Jamie kept a diary, and he often wrote in it. These words, perhaps, summed up his philosophy and attitude towards life, as well as his perspective on the escape that climbing allowed for: 'All I can see is how dysfunctional society is, at least in my view. Mountain life is such a contrast, not just the lack of people, but the pace of time and the priority of things. The way things are in the mountains, all in the present moment, is what I strive for in city life. Suddenly when I step back into civilisation I realise all too quickly why [that] is so hard to achieve. There are so many distractions and every decision suddenly has a million variables. I know this because in the supermarket I wander from aisle to aisle dazed and confused, whereas in the mountains everything is so much clearer and simpler. Nature dictates decisions and I fall into the natural rhythm of my surrounds.'

Reading those words, especially with our expedition being so close, I tried to find perspective on where my own pathway might lead. And, then, what it was about the mountains that provided a balance to my life.

Jamie's writing reminded me of the clarity of purpose that mountaineering could provide: to be challenged by a self-imposed obstacle, to hopefully reach the pinnacle, and then to be able to make the decision to return. To carry on.

It never gets any easier losing someone close, regardless of how they died. And, for a long time, I didn't want to think about the mountains or about climbing. And certainly not about committing to an expedition to Nepal. I didn't really know how we reached a decision to buy the tickets. Even now, I'm not entirely sure. I think maybe it became part of the grieving process. Just trying to carry on as normal, when you know that nothing will be the same. *Do it. Fill the void with something. Anything. Breathe.*

And we did. Within a few weeks of losing two close friends to mountaineering accidents at opposite ends of the earth, we had committed to trying to climb Anidesha Chuli. You wouldn't be wrong in pointing out the potential foolhardiness of such a decision, especially at that particular time and given my state of mind.

Whenever I felt like I was losing my way, and especially if mountains didn't provide the answer, I would return to the sea. I had grown up close to the ocean, and through my youth, I became at home immersing myself in it as often as possible.

Like so often before, the beach and the ocean and the waves—of course, the waves—became the source of my unbridling. The ocean acted as my confidant, my shrink. There, I felt more confident. More in control of the what ifs that had been keeping me awake night after night. Some mornings I would lie in bed and think *What the fuck am I doing? Can I even be any more inconsiderate and selfish? The fucking mountains will kill everything and everyone that I love if I let them.* The sea doesn't require so much from me.

Clumps of seaweed formed jumbled islands on the wet sand, but I barely registered their random, sometimes hulking presence. My mind was fuddled with snow slopes and avalanches and karabiners and ropes and tents and altitude sickness pills...and with loss. It needed a thorough saltwater cleansing.

Seeing clumps of seaweed in the early morning light made me think of Shelley. She liked to jump on the tiny teardrops attached to the seaweed, which made plopping noises as she stomped down. *Plop. Plop. Plop-plop.* It always took us ages to walk along a beach whenever a storm had dumped another load of the ever-alluring, un-plopped seaweed in front of us. Sometimes other beachgoers tried not to stare at the jumping weirdo. In return, Shelley pretended not to notice them. She just stomped and stomped. It made me laugh and love my wife all the more.

This morning, Shelley was still in bed, curled up with our two cats Tommy and George. No doubt she was dreaming of ice-crusted summits. She's mentally much tougher than I am; she was born with a stubborn streak that has dragged her to the top of most things more often than not. I'm happy to draft along in the wake of her single-minded drive, and to make sure we have the best chance of getting off the mountain again. I'm especially good at the part where we go down. *Home is that way.*

One of the largest clumps of seaweed nearby grunted and sighed. In the half-light, I almost crapped myself. *Bloody things's alive! Christ! It's a leopard seal!*

Best described as a monster zapped straight from Dinosaur

Land, leopard seals usually hang out down in the Antarctic. These sleek killers plunder cute little penguins and smaller seals for dinner and harass anything that pisses them off. This guy was a long way from home.

After giving a sudden wide berth to my new acquaintance, I paused. Clearly it wasn't threatened by my presence, and neither should it have been. Built like a streamlined tank, and with jaws and teeth set to tear and pulverise, I couldn't imagine it getting flustered by much at all.

Was the leopard seal a boy or a girl? Maybe a girl as it seemed pretty sleek, not that I knew much about leopard seals other than that over the years they'd killed a few people—I think the last time was the drowning of a female scientist who was scuba diving under the ice. Presumably being overly friendly, the leopard seal held her down until she eventually ran out of air while being a mammal's play toy.

Obviously, death waits for us along a myriad of paths, some chosen, some as random as a twist of unluckiness—even some, it seems, with a bloody leopard seal! The choosing is not a death wish, but rather a conscious decision about action and consequence, and even more fundamentally about the essential worth of risk in our lives. Marty and Jamie were a constant reminder with every decision I faced and would face on the mountain we were going to climb.

I could so easily have lost Shelley during the terrifying earthquakes that devastated Christchurch, or one of my best mates Graham under what seemed like a skip-load of falling ice a few months later on Rabbiters Peak. I wondered how much fight, and breath, I'd had left when my leg rope recently snapped in heavy surf off the coast of Otago, and I'd barely made it to shore against the current and turbulence. I'd sat on the wet sand, purging saltwater from my lungs until I could breathe properly again. My previous confidence in the ocean had almost been shattered by a single experience.

Our upcoming flight to Nepal was with Malaysia Airlines, a company with a solid safety record yet which had somehow managed to completely lose one of its planes with 239 people on board. It's funny what your mind fleetingly registers when you almost trip over an unexpected predator lurking like a clump of un-plopped seaweed on your home beach.

The mountain we were attempting to climb was given the nickname White Wave by visiting westerners. The name appealed to me. It seemed appropriate. From the valley, the mountain loomed like the last in a huge set on an outer reef far from shore. Difficult to reach. And enticing because of that difficulty.

I'd spent hours pouring over photos from the unsuccessful attempt of a previous expedition, and then talking to the climbers involved. I was trying to consider every contingency like I tended to overdo. Trying to ascertain the mood of a mountain is difficult when it's so far away from home.

Everything about Anidesha Chuli seemed different. Strange. Foreign. But, I guess, that was part of the allure. The separation would be so much greater given the mountain's strangeness; to be successful, we had to engage fully.

The paths we choose versus the paths that are chosen for us. Sometimes I struggle to accept that fate plays its hand regardless of my insecurities or need to overanalyse, and I'm better off just getting on with it.

The leopard seal opened one eye to look at me. Then it sniffed the air, before shuffling its powerful body further into the sand. One long flipper hiffed a flipper-full of sand in my general direction, in what could easily be interpreted as a dismissive gesture. *You are no threat.*

Slowly the gloom lifted, both from the coming day and from the dark recess of my mind. I could see white water folding around the point farther down the beach. Sweet! The swell had hung around.

Here comes that warm feeling inside that I'd been looking for, a wee spark of 'go get it' that helps to drag me out of bed each morning. To rise before dawn. To face the light of the coming day like it's my first and could be my last. To embrace the fleeting nature of us. The White Wave awaits.

NINETEEN

'The slower you go the further you get,' Alex the Russian said to me.

Lanky, loud, and with a seemingly eternal grin, Alex was part of a large international team attempting the North face of Kanchenchunga. At 8586 metres, this is the world's third-highest mountain (New Zealander Norman Hardie was on the mountain's first ascent back in 1955).

Alex and I kept crossing paths during the ten-day trek from Taplejung, the last town near the end of the road in eastern Nepal, as we followed the tumble and froth of the Ghunsa River into the heart of the Himalaya. I certainly appreciated the big Russian's advice. Being a slow acclimatiser, it seemed an appropriate motto for me to adopt for our own expedition.

Our objective was at the head of the Ramdang Valley, near the border with India and China, and not far from the base camp for Kanchenchunga's northern aspect. When I told Alex that we had plenty of beer and wine—but, alas, no vodka—he still suggested coming to visit our camp during a break from his climbing.

Altitude slowly increased as I passed through fields of rice and cardamon in the lower Tamor Valley. I wandered beneath flowering rhododendron forests and skirted stroppy-looking water buffalo and yaks. I refilled my water bottle at each side stream, peered through thick clumps of bamboo in the hope of glimpsing a rare red panda, and I called out 'Namaste' to every smiling Nepalese that passed by on the trail.

Absorbing through smell, sound, and sight as much as I could of such a remote and incredibly beautiful corner of the world, I realised that overloading my senses like this was a huge part of what enticed me to invest so much time, energy, and money into overseas expeditions.

And then, of course, there were the mountains. They rose sharply, castles of ice and stone, monoliths so imposing that, before considering to climb them, I must first look down at the earth and focus on placing one foot in front of the other. But that's the nature of risk and reward, isn't it? The initial step, and surely the step that really matters, is in the choosing to try.

I was here with Shelley, our good friend John, and our base camp support staff from Dream Himalaya Adventures, all of us hoping that the snow conditions, the weather, and our ability to cope with the altitude aligned enough for us to be successful. I have always loved, or at least appreciated, the knowledge that adventure arises about the same time that the certainty of outcome vanishes.

This was John's first expedition. John is a strapping red-headed Australian, and we had instantly hit it off while working together at Bivouac Outdoor in Christchurch. John was working the day of the major earthquake, and I remember our support for each other and for those around us during the aftermath. His calmness during the natural disaster was just one of the reasons why I thought he would make a great climbing partner.

Before heading to Nepal, John and I did some mountaineering trips together back in New Zealand. One particular trip comes to mind: we were spending our first night at Barker Hut, in Arthur's Pass National Park, when all of a sudden John started moaning and thrashing around in the top bunk.

'Ugggh fnkkkk thnnnng!'

Not knowing what in God's name was happening up there, I considered whether I should keep pretending to read my book, dash outside, or offer assistance. Eventually, curiosity got the better of me, and I glanced up from my copy of *Man Alone*.

'Mate, are you okay?'

John was shoving himself against the corner of the hut so hard that the veins on his neck pulsed. Both of his legs were also sticking out at odd angles from under his sleeping bag.

'Ccccrrraaammmmpp!'

'That does look uncomfortable. Maybe...maybe, if you stretch your legs...'

'I'mmm friggennn ttrrryying!'

It was one of those weird situations: here was a friend obviously in pain, and I couldn't do anything to help. I felt bad because of it, yet all I wanted to do was laugh at John's facial contortions. Having in the past experienced what he was going through, I figured laughing might not help.

John put up quite a struggle. At times, the whole hut shook with his convulsions, and I was impressed by his stamina. Unfortunately, John's cramp continued off and on through the night, and neither of us got much sleep.

By the next morning, my friend appeared, understandably, pretty worn out.

'Maybe we should have a hut day,' I suggested.

'Bugger that,' John replied. 'Let's go climbing!'

In his book *Mountains of the Mind*, British author Robert Macfarlane explains how sublime landscapes, like the one I was experiencing for the first time in East Nepal, can reshape 'our understanding of ourselves...In their vastness and in their intricacy, mountains stretch out the individual mind and compress it simultaneously...make it aware of its own immeasurable acreage and reach and, at the same time, of its own smallness'.

Normally, I treasure the opportunity of connecting any mountain with my mind-scape. I love it when the curved edges of snow merge softly into a thin cloud rising from the valleys until one can't be distinguished from the other. It's as if I'm awake in the middle of a dream.

But other mountains can rise upwards like a nightmare might from the valley fog. Ice shields carry the sheen and texture of white steel. Rock appears without feature, bulging impossibly at an altitude where even the gentlest of angles would provide enough challenge. Before these mountains, instead of some luminous, romantic vision of self-discovery, an aspiring climber might more readily imagine annihilation— or else, total transformation—of their consciousness if not themselves.

During our trek into the Base Camp for Anidesha Chuli, I

was about to set eyes on such a mountain.

I figured I couldn't have been far from the settlement of Kambachen, near the head of the Ramdang Valley. Up the side of an old moraine wall, the track turned back on itself. There was the hushing of wind as it glided over the highlands, the sound of water trickling nearby, and laughter echoing from somewhere above or below me.

I leaned against a boulder to rest. Looking up for the first time in a while, suddenly I caught sight of a newly revealed vista that, as French climber Guido Magnone wrote some five decades earlier, 'consists entirely of horrific hanging glaciers and vertical snow-cluttered walls'.

Before me rose the 3000-metre-high North face of Jannu— the great Kumbhakarna that I had read and wondered so much about—surely one of the most daunting alpine walls on earth. I started giggling nervously. Then I struggled to breathe. With its darkened shoulders hunched beneath a cloak of clouds, the mountain before me appeared without niceties, a demeanour solely, and very obviously, of immense threat. There was no doubt as to its mood.

The absurdity of the situation made me laugh all the harder. I had to slump to the ground to regather my breath. The first view of an iconic mountain is supposed to be awe-inspiring. As a climber, I should have felt my thirst for adventure aroused. But, the apparition before me seemed only to clasp together all of the insecurities that haunted me from previous failures and to forebode one that I was yet to experience that same season.

In mountaineering, and explored throughout mountain literature, there is nearly always an underlying question of what is possible and what is not. Of what is acceptable versus unacceptable risk. Somehow that question felt keener, or at least more readily answered, with my first sight of Jannu. The mountain looked beyond my ability. I didn't even want to think about climbing it.

While I rested beneath Jannu in the late morning sun, feeling slightly dazed from the altitude and what I had seen, a local man passed by. Heading down the valley, he paused and smiled. With an incline of his head and a slight frown, he seemed to be enquiring whether I was okay. I grinned and then nodded, and he continued on.

For a foreigner, the experience of an overland road trip from Kathmandu to Taplejung, in the far east of Nepal, is something akin to riding inside one of those mechanical bucking bulls found in the American rodeos. So potholed and ruptured is the narrow, winding road that one can't avoid becoming overly jarred and rattled and shaken...for two full days.

From the capital's elevated plateau, the road descends south to the plains linking Nepal with India. This land is hot and dry, and seemingly a world away from the cold ceiling of the world only some 100 kilometres to the north. Views of white giants might be glimpsed on the horizon until, eventually, the journey eases back northwards towards them.

Heading up, over and around the steep foothills of the Himalaya of East Nepal, many of which are planted with the famous Ilam tea, the road drops and climbs, winds, and jinks some more, before finally—thankfully—arriving at its conclusion, the mountain town of Taplejung.

This is the most eastern district of Nepal, with the border to India around thirty-five kilometres to the east, and China fifty kilometres to the north. The backbones of high mountain ranges arch impressively in all directions. And beneath them, great, flowing rivers carve their paths through steep-walled valleys, eventually on to the plains. A land of extremes, there are monsoonal floods in summer and blankets of snow in winter. Life here, especially for the locals who live at a higher altitude, can be rudimentary and full of hardship.

Before the existence of the road, early mountain expeditions used to travel into this region from India rather than Kathmandu. First organising in the town of Darjeeling—a place also famous for its tea—long foot-trains of porters and sahibs would take to the narrow trails leading into the mysterious and alluring mountains to the west, gone from their homelands for many months at a time.

After the two-day bus ride, we were certainly keen to start hiking. With our staff Ang Nima, Sangay, and Tenzin Sherpa Jorden, and twenty porters carrying around 700kgs of food and equipment for Base Camp, we followed the Ghunsa River into the heart of the Himalaya. We passed through small villages, farmland, and forest. Sometimes we stayed close to the river, crossing narrow wire bridges over tight gorges, and other times we climbed steeply up to high terraces that allowed views of the mountains ahead. Our anticipation grew with every step. To say we were amping would be an understatement!

John became unwell at Sekathum. Initially, he complained of a stomach bug, but it soon deteriorated to a very high resting pulse, high fever, continuous vomiting, diarrhoea and delirium. Despite giving John antibiotics from our medical kit, he was too sick to move for a number of days.

At one stage, Shelley and I discussed whether John might need to be evacuated. As each day passed without our friend improving, and to keep the trip progressing (partly to ensure we didn't lose our porters and gear!), Shelley and I decided that I would need to leave the two of them and go on ahead with Ang Nima. We hugged, knowing that if John didn't recover then Shelley would likely have to fly out with him. If this happened, we would be days and miles apart, and possibly wouldn't see each other again until back in New Zealand.

Before leaving the others, I made a final satellite phone call to Dr. Dick Price, an acquaintance in New Zealand, for more advice on helping John. Dick is an experienced expedition doctor and, after listening to my uneducated diagnosis of John's symptoms, he politely suggested a change of antibiotics. Luckily, the different medication worked over the next few days. Under the watchful eye of Shelley, John started to regather his health, and then his strength.

Upon hearing the news of John's recovery, I waited at Kambachen, the last small summer settlement. Once John and Shelley arrived at Kambachen, the three of us continued together up the side valley Ramdang to the site where we would set up a camp for the climb.

The long, slow height gain from Kambachen, which included seeing fresh snow leopard prints on the track we were following, saw us establish Base Camp on the moraine rubble of the Ramdang Glacier at around 4800 metres. The most suitable site, it still offered plenty of visual excitement, with countless rock falls careering off the moraine walls above us, and the occasional collapsing seracs from high summits to the south. We tried to convince each other and ourselves that no flying missiles should be able to reach our tent sites—not quite, at least!

So far, the weather had been mostly stable, and any afternoon cloud that bubbled up from the valley brought little wind or snowfall with it. Everyone was feeling rested and relatively comfortable at the altitude, especially John, who, by now, had made what seemed a full recovery. Even I felt like I had acclimatised to the altitude. So, as soon as possible, the three of us jammed our packs with essential food and climbing equipment, said goodbye to our Base Camp staff, and set off for our first acclimatising climb.

After a few hours of slowly gaining height, we found a suitable site on the glacier for Camp 1. At around 5200 metres, we were now underneath the main icefall leading up to Anidesha Chuli. A huge cirque of mountains rose above us, most of which looked rather difficult, if not too dangerous, to ascend. We had been warned by the previous team that the icefall access to the upper névé of Anidesha Chuli was broken and complicated to negotiate. So we were not surprised by what we were faced with.

Later in the day, by the time we had erected our tents, I started to feel the first affects of Acute Mountain Sickness (AMS). My breathing became rapid and shallow, my pulse grew rapid, and I had developed a bad headache. Shelley suggested that I should get into my sleeping bag inside the tent to rest. Curled up in my warm cocoon, I willed my symptoms to ease.

But they didn't. Over the next two hours, my condition deteriorated to the point of suspected High Altitude Cerebral Edema (HACE). My headache was getting much worse and I started to lose the ability to think coherently. I can't recall too much of what happened next. Shelley told me afterwards that she had asked me whether we should go down, but apparently I said that I didn't want to because I couldn't work out how to put my boots on.

Although I was typically a slow acclimatiser, this was the first time I had been this sick at altitude. John and Shelley rightly decided that they needed to try and get me back down to our Base Camp as quickly as possible, in case I deteriorated further. Shelley tied the laces of my boots, and the two of them helped me to my feet. I was unsteady and disorientated, but I could still walk slowly whichever direction I was pointed in. Over the next few hours, the others helped me down the glacier, and we arrived back at Base Camp just before dark.

With the loss of altitude, my condition stabilised enough that I managed to rest that night. Given that my worst symptoms had eased by the next morning, John and Shelley decided that they could safely leave me with our staff and continue their acclimatising. They headed back up the glacier to our tent, before pushing through the icefall to a site for Camp 2 at around 5400 metres.

Snow conditions were poor through the icefall, with unconsolidated drifts up to thigh deep, and little visibility due to low cloud. The following morning Shelley and John continued up to 5600 metres, sometimes forcing through waist-deep snow (at one stage a 90 metre height gain took over two hours). When a thunderstorm hit, followed by heavy snowfall, the pair rightly decided to retreat back to Base Camp.

Over the next week, the weather remained poor, with strong winds and snow falling every day at our camp. There was already dubious snowpack stability, and we were concerned that the extra snowfall was only exacerbating conditions. Numerous avalanches were seen and heard on the lee slopes above camp. The forecast for the following week was for more of the same.

To help pass the time, Shelley, John, and I taught Tenzin

and Sangay how to climb on a steep curve of glacial ice just above Base Camp. Their keenness to master the techniques of using ice axe and crampons helped remind me that our journey shouldn't be just about focusing on our own, selfish goals. It was rewarding to see them progress so quickly.

Tenzin told me that he believed the growing number of western visitors was a boon for the Tamor Valley. Where once in his village there was only subsistence farming and occasional trade with Tibetans from over the high mountain passes nearby, tourism had grown to become the most important source of income for the locals. From my perspective, the main settlement of Ghunsa and its residents were certainly a welcome respite from the long trail into the mountains.

However, I also knew that, in some other areas of Nepal, the high number of visitors had threatened the delicate environmental balance of the mountains by inadvertently destroying plant and animal life and by leaving behind a growing quantity of refuse. Studying the mostly pristine landscape around us, I hoped this type of negative impact, often associated with increasing tourism, wouldn't also become the case in the Tamor Valley.

We estimated that at least six days would be required to climb and descend Anidesha Chuli. With time running out, especially due to the ongoing unsettled weather, I suggested to the others that perhaps I should remain at Base Camp on any future attempt. Hopefully this would allow a higher chance of success as John and Shelley were moving much more efficiently at altitude.

While I was personally disappointed at this decision, it seemed the right thing to do for the team. I was also concerned by how quickly I had deteriorated on the previous gain in altitude. If I had become unconscious at Camp 1, or while John and Shelley were trying to help me back to Base Camp, then there was a reasonable chance I wouldn't have made it back down at all.

John and Shelley decided to attempt a climb as soon as there was another break in the weather. One fine afternoon, they returned to Camp 1 to spend the night. It snowed that evening, but the next morning was clear, so they pushed up towards 5700 metres, trying to find a way through the icefall to reach the upper névé. But again they were faced with unconsolidated snow, sometimes chest deep now, and they were unable to navigate the next tier of icefall in deteriorating visibility. Another storm hit that afternoon with even more snowfall, and they decided that the safest option—the only real option—was to abandon the climb.

In hindsight, and despite major disappointment amongst the three of us at the time, it was clearly the right decision to descend from the mountain. Conditions higher on Anidesha Chuli would likely have been much worse than what John and Shelley experienced at 5600—5700 metres.

Later, we found out that it had been a particularly high snowfall season across the Himalaya, with increased avalanche risk in most of the popular climbing areas. And, indeed, tragedies on both Everest and Kanchenjunga (both due to avalanches) further illustrated just how risky things were during the season.

I have mixed feelings thinking back to this expedition. Mostly, I guess, I feel regret that we weren't successful. Despite the added factors of John getting sick, and then me not being able to cope with the altitude, the trip still felt like a failure.

But there are other things to consider. Trying to climb Anidesha Chuli was an important part of the journey, but it was still only one part. The story of travelling to and into the heart of the mountains was multilayered, interwoven with learning about local culture and customs, and growing an appreciation for the land that was measured much more than by what summit we may or may not have been able to reach.

After walking back down the valley, again I had a chance to consider the impact that Jannu and the other mountains had on me as a climber as well as on the local region and its inhabitants. The alluring and dark sublime of particular summits could be interpreted as a protective presence, in the way the locals chose to view them. I found it reassuring how the people here also designated moods to their more favoured summits.

The existence of Jannu—Kumbhakarna, the sleeping warrior—and how locals lived and breathed so humbly within its shadow, these were guiding principles to how deeply this place should rest in my heart. There is a responsibility that comes with travelling and exploring and climbing in places such as these. We should always be aware of our potential impact, and we should show respect.

Perhaps, after suffering from AMS and HACE, I might have descended to Kambachen for a few days to recover at a lower altitude before returning to help the others if I could. Certainly, if the weather had been more stable that season, it was something I would likely have considered.

When looking back at various factors of the trip from the comfort of my living room, it is easy enough to reason that I might not have been in the right state of mind for that climb. Perhaps I was still grieving the loss of Jamie and Marty. And especially so when I was doing something that exposed me and those I loved to the same risky activity that had claimed the lives of my two friends. My sudden deterioration in health only added to an underlying lack of self-belief in my climbing ability.

John had done well on his first expedition, especially after his sickness, and Shelley was as strong and reliable as always at altitude. But it seemed like I had contributed little to the expedition. I felt like a failure.

I recall stepping onto the plane at Kathmandu, to fly back to New Zealand, and wondering if I would ever want to try another overseas expedition. A part of me also wondered whether, at that moment, I wanted to do any more mountain climbing at all.

TWENTY

A bed of warm, flat granite, with the sun sliding into the Tasman Sea and a red sky slowly fading to blue-black. Then the same place the following night, the rock now cold to touch and our exposed bivouac site trapped by a foreboding cloud that encroaches from above and below.

After returning from Nepal, I didn't climb in the mountains for two years. The decision to stop felt sudden, as if, after getting home, I instantly went, 'that's it'. But, really, it wasn't. Possibly, it wasn't even a conscious decision. More so, there had been an ongoing separation of my goals and motivations from the risks that mountaineering had been exposing me to. There was an osmosis of different ideals slowly leading me away from the all-or-nothing world that existed up high, a world that had drawn me to focus on it at the expense of other things in my life for so long. A commitment that had, at times, cost so much.

Did climbing leave me or did I leave her? Did it even matter what the relationship had meant in the past or who moved on from the other first? I told myself I was done. There would be no more freezing nights trying to sleep on hard, uneven ground. No more heavy packs and endless uphills. No more God-awful starts in the dark, with numbed fingers and toes, and a twist in my gut that I still can't decide whether was guided by apprehension or anticipation. No more walls of rock that, while I told myself they were okay, really were piles of choss. No more unreliable weather. No more struggling to find a way down in the cloud and the dark and the cold. No more being scared when nothing's even happened. And, perhaps most importantly, no more loss.

I had decided I was done with the risk, happy to replace climbing mountains with focussing on building a new home, taking up mountain biking, more surfing and a gentle, semi-dignified slide into the advanced middle years. There had been just too many close calls to justify continuing. Yep, I was over it!

I had managed to convince myself it was okay to step away. Making the call to give up climbing was the right thing to do. I was approaching an age where altitude taxed my body too much. It was time to retire.

The separation still felt like a jolt, realising I had reached the end of a three-decade relationship. Like there was now a part of me missing, and I couldn't quite make up my mind whether it was a good thing or not. I felt different—totally different—a little empty inside, and sometimes scrambling to fill the new abyss with the things that *other* people might do. The volume had been turned down on my emotions. My new normal seemed a bit dull.

But that was okay. The way I felt was to be expected. Making a clean break required commitment and the ability to modify my expectations. Hopefully, the feeling of dullness would recede. After all, climbing had taught me to deal with whatever adversity lay before me. I knew how to plan and adapt. I knew how to suffer if necessary. I was prepared to accept the consequences.

Yet there I was, laying in bed at home at 4:00 a.m. one morning, suddenly wide awake and thinking about climbing. It must have been a dream that woke me. Or something in the dream, something unsettling that, of course, I couldn't recall more than a few fragments of as soon as I woke. Sometimes, in my climbing dreams, I remember only falling or flying. It's pretty easy to work out which one's the better dream. But this dream was different. There was the sea and walls of rock and a feeling of desperation. And why, after lurching awake, did I feel so guilty about something that I couldn't remember?

I woke with a distinct impression that I had made a bad decision. Lying there in the dark, it took a while to work out that the decision had to do with climbing. It felt like I had betrayed myself as well as the memories of others. *Get a grip!* There was a good reason, or a bunch of them, that had made me decide to ease back from climbing. Past experiences. Maybe something pivotal in the dream, if only I could remember.

The dream also left me feeling reflective, and somewhat nostalgic, for days afterwards. I decided that I needed to sort out what was important in my life, just to be sure I'd made the right decision. What really mattered.

Before choosing to give up climbing, I had been dividing most of my time between it, surfing, and writing. I loved sharing the varied experiences with Shelley and a few close friends. There seemed no order or balance to my priorities, but each experience felt like it meshed succinctly into the whole. There was a mix of randomness of events here, a few lucky choices there, and I found myself in the middle age and well along the journey—towards what, I wasn't entirely sure. But that's life, and more specifically the way of risk and reward, isn't it? Of act and consequence.

Adventure starts around the same time as uncertainty. Letting go is the first step. It's the beginning of a journey that some of us choose to take, and I knew that I'd rather take it consciously than be dragged along by an innate acceptance of what might have been. Did I now doubt my decision to stop climbing?

When people asked me what I did with my time, I replied that I wrote for a living. I realised that it was a programmed response, as if my work was the most important thing to focus on. When you think about it, it seems a funny thing to say. What do I do? I did—and still do—many things. Some are central to my life and others are just a means of getting by. Other than providing the ability to earn money, work may or may not fit into that category. Surely the question to ask myself is: *What do I look forward to doing?*

With my writing work, I appreciated that I got the opportunity to explore and then write about our environment, about how fragile and essential it is. I thanked my lucky stars for my life, my wife, and the path I was on. And I tried to remind myself of this every day.

I had felt the same way with my experiences climbing in the mountains. When I hadn't escaped to the hills for a time, or when the weather forced cancelled trip after cancelled trip, I'd find myself losing touch with the feelings that mountaineering induced. I began to imagine that I wasn't capable enough anymore. I started to lack confidence in my previous ability to pack accurately, move efficiently, and make safe decisions in an unforgiving environment.

No amount of local cragging or hill running would keep me prepared. I was forced to scan maps longingly, pour over guidebook photos and route descriptions, telling myself that the bad weather wouldn't always fall on weekends. Sooner or later, I'd get to test myself in the high wilds once again. I yearned for the satisfied ache that came from blurred hours hauling a pack jammed with climbing paraphernalia. I wanted to clear the cobwebs of too many morning-tea flat whites, escape the small towers of dirty dishes from three nights ago, and poke the proverbial at all vicarious living associated with staring into a box of moving pictures for the answers that were more likely to be found within myself.

Yeah, *not* climbing made me bitter. I got grumpy that the weather wouldn't work around me, when four months passed between trips, and when I felt more familiar packing and unpacking my ice axes than actually swinging them into an unsuspecting but otherwise appropriate blob of polystyrene ice hidden somewhere high on a frozen mountainside.

All of these thoughts and emotions occupied my mind in the days following the dream. And, I guess this is where the real crux of my story exists: Why did the passion for challenging myself in the mountains start to diminish? And then, after an extended time away from climbing, what instigated the realisation that I needed to find a pathway back? To be true to what I really desired.

I didn't want my climbing to stop. I had just needed a reset of how to approach it and what I wanted to achieve.

The opening line in the poem Place by New Zealand poet Brian Turner comes to mind: 'Once in a while you may come across a place where everything seems as close to perfection as you will ever need.' Certain physical aspects, or environs, create the opportunity for us to find happiness and feelings of inner contentment. Seeking ways to interact, if we can, are essential to creating the opportunity to grow within ourselves.

How could I start again? After two years away, I felt completely out of touch. My fitness was poor and my headspace probably unreliable.

It would be like facing the crux of a climb, I told myself. *Don't get bogged down by all of the mental baggage. Trust in the doing.* After all, uncertainty was part of the attraction. And, yes, I understood only too well what Jamie and Marty would have been saying to me!

Finding the way back. Something to inspire me again. Something new.

But to do that I needed to work through what had been hindering me. I needed to face up to finally accepting that Jamie and Marty and other friends had died doing an activity that they loved, and that I loved but also agonised—rightly or wrongly—over the worth of. My tendency to overanalyse helped to keep me safe, but sometimes it also held me back.

That's the dichotomy of my relationship with climbing, the quandary I found myself in. I had developed a tendency to be so cautious, while still trying to be successful doing something that required total commitment. At some stage, I needed to let go.

'We need to focus less on goals or endpoints and more on the process or journey. No one is going to care what climbs I did or didn't do when I pass away—they'll remember the experiences they had with me.'

These words were written by Jamie back in 2008. Jamie could be a great philosopher at times, about life, about family, the future, and the world as he saw it. Jamie had goals, and he formed plans on how to reach those goals.

What is it that brings solace to each individual? What building blocks do we need to feel whole in ourselves? Surely it is for each of us to decide, as long as it doesn't harm others. For me, being alone in the mountains feels like being alone at sea. There is space and the opportunity for calmness. An internal cadence takes over. Everything becomes so much simpler. I breathe and move. I rest when I need to. I live.

The realisation set in. I definitely needed to find a pathway back. But finding a pathway back also meant recognising what I had forgotten or lost touch with. Eventually, the feeling would return. My intuition for the mountains would rekindle itself.

In my mind, the summit still beckoned. Hidden behind bushy outcrops and rocky spurs, its final broad snowy peak felt just as elusive. But, for me, it wasn't so much the summit that I was yearning for anymore. It was the process of getting there, the external challenge and internal strengthening. It was the familiarity of escape, and then of finding myself within that escape.

Focus on the joy I feel in the doing. I wanted to do that. But, sometimes, my fear held me back. A fear of what? Sure, I'd get scared before a climb and sometimes at particularly challenging moments during it. But that wasn't an all-consuming, paralysing fear. I was familiar with fear and knew how to deal with it.

And I wasn't fearful of *actually* dying. I didn't *want* to die, obviously, but I wasn't afraid of it. So what then?

Perhaps it was something as simple as wanting to make the safest decisions all of the time. I had put too much pressure on myself to get everything right. But, of course, there are too many variables in the mountains to get my decisions right on every climb.

Was it something else then? And, if so, what?

I needed a new perspective. Some other view, or views, to help reframe what I had been struggling to decipher.

TWENTY-ONE

The last time I had seen Sequoia Schmidt, she was knee-high to a grasshopper. It would have been 1994 or 1995. I was probably supposed to be studying for exams at university, and no doubt Sequoia was trying to undo the knots in a rope that her father, Marty, tied around her so he and I could climb a nearby rock face unhindered for a few more minutes.

Meeting Sequoia again more than two decades later, at the New Zealand Mountain Film and Book Festival in Wanaka, felt almost like fate. Not quite—because I don't really believe in fate—but almost.

I didn't know Sequoia was going to be at the festival, so it was a great surprise to bump into her. Once we had made the connection, Sequoia was bubbly and forthright. She had her father's easy smile and his same ability to engage with people. We hugged. We laughed. Finding a quiet space in a nearby cafe, we sat and talked about Marty and how much influence he had exerted over both of our lives.

We also talked about Marty and Denali's deaths. I was particularly interested in hearing how the K2 climb and accident had affected Sequoia. For me, this sharing of our experiences and feelings was an act of catharsis that had been long overdue. Perhaps it was for Sequoia as well.

Sunday night usually meant dinner at Sequoia's grandfather's home whenever she was staying in Houston, Texas.

'The night before the dinner, I had this weird feeling that something might be wrong,' Sequoia said to me. 'So, I messaged a close friend of my dad's [Lance Machovsky] and asked if there was somewhere I could follow what was happening with the K2 climb that Dad and Denali were on. Then Lance explained that they were currently missing on the mountain.'

It's fair to say that Sequoia's relationship with her father had been strained for many years. This could be put down to a number of factors—including her parent's separation when she was young, as well as Marty not being present enough when Sequoia needed him as she grew older.

While being estranged from her father, Sequoia still kept in close contact with Denali. And she had known about the expedition and planned attempt to climb K2.

'I guess I just brushed off the worry initially,' Sequoia explained. 'Of course, Dad had been on so many expeditions. I woke up the next morning and, like normal, went over to my grandfather's place.'

On this particular Sunday—July 28, 2013—Sequoia's phone rang twice during the evening meal, but she decided to ignore it. Then she got a text. 'I remember it really vividly. I was walking up the stairs after dinner when Lance texted me. "Call me back ASAP." So I immediately did. And all Lance said to me in that moment was that there had been an avalanche and it was presumed that Marty and Denali were dead.'

Shock is an instinctive response designed to shield or protect us, for example, from the sudden pain of loss. Like taking a sedative, we are numbed. Thoughts become blurred or hazy. There may be disbelief, or a sudden lapse of memory.

The deep cut of grief is still to come. Through the following days and weeks, the intenseness may—and in my experience, usually does—feel like there is no way through it. Emotions rise in waves. Anger. Sadness. Guilt. Resentment. Loneliness. Regret. It is believed that we need to go through these different stages of grief to reach a point of realisation. Acceptance, if it ever comes, is usually right at the end.

But, at least for a moment, the shock shields us.

For Sequoia, most of the next period of time passed in a blur. 'After the phone call from Lance, for the next hour I was just crying,' she said. 'Then I picked up the phone and called my Aunt and Uncle, and after that, I called some of our childhood friends to let them know as well.'

Sequoia recalled being conflicted emotionally. 'I was really angry at Dad because Denali wouldn't have been on that mountain if it wasn't for him. But then I was also angry at myself for not having healed or repaired my relationship with Dad. Now it was too late to do anything about it.'

Sequoia then travelled to her other grandparent's [Marty's

parents] home which was in Castro Valley, California, and she stayed with them for a few days.

'There was a whole bunch of Dad's climbing equipment stored in the basement of their house,' she said. 'I remember sticking my nose in his duffle bag of gear and just smelling it, like a longing sensation to have some kind of a connection.'

What followed for Sequoia was a particularly challenging time coping with the loss of her brother and her father, but also having to deal with various ongoing conflicts with Marty's extended family. 'The funny thing is, when you have torn relationships, just because you go through a traumatic situation like loss doesn't mean those relationships are going to be mended,' she said to me. 'I stayed with my Dad's parents, thinking our relationship was all okay now. We were bonding over grief. But it only lasted about four days, and then erupted into a huge fight.'

The conflict ensued around what memorials Sequoia was and wasn't allowed to attend. There was also contention over the conditions of the will, especially in terms of Marty's climbing equipment, which Sequoia understood had been left to her. In the end, most of the gear was sold without her consent.

'The first time I saw some of his gear again was when I was climbing the Northwest ridge of Mount Aspiring. I was staying in the hut, and another climber had a sleeping bag and an ice axe with MSIG [Marty Schmidt International Guiding) written on it. Sometime after that, in Nepal, there was a duffel bag with MSIG on it, and then at Aconcagua Base Camp [in South America] there was a tent. Over the years, it became a really awesome feeling. Instead of me being angry about it, I was getting to see a small part of him everywhere, in different mountains around the world.'

Marty once told me that Sequoia was on her own path in life. I can't recall the whole conversation, or what instigated it, but I remember Marty saying how proud he was of her as well as Denali. 'She knows what she wants and no one is going to stop her getting it,' he had said. Marty also explained at the time that he was hopeful of being able to repair his relationship with Sequoia one day. Despite giving her whatever space she required, it was important to him to connect again.

I was aware that the Schmidt family life, unorthodox in many ways, had been challenging. Sequoia, in particular, had a difficult upbringing. Marty could be away for months at a time with his work climbing.

'Everyone makes the assumption that I was really mad at my Dad because he was gone all the time,' Sequoia said. 'But that's not the case. Not at all. I think if there had been a stable environment at home, if I had had a mother who was normal, if I had a support system, and if I wasn't in and out of foster care, then I would have felt very differently towards my father. The anger wasn't because he was gone.'

Sequoia's need for the stability her father hadn't been able to provide drove a wedge between them. But, Sequoia understood.

'For me, part of the grief process is also the acceptance,' she said. 'And, part of acceptance is the realisation that this could happen to any one of us at any time in our lives regardless of what risks we are taking. So if we're all going to die, no matter what we do in life, then why stop something that you enjoy doing and that helps you grow as a person?'

Sequoia understood what it meant to pursue something that you loved, no matter what the cost was. She recognised the reasons why Marty was away so often, why he made the choices that he did.

'If Dad had chosen to stop mountaineering, and instead be a tradesman and miserable but be there for me every day, I would swap that in a heartbeat for having a father that was gone,' she said. 'Because, when Dad was there, he instilled in me a passion and drive and inspiration to do what I want to do. I cherish that memory far more so now.'

Sequoia is a competent climber, but her main adventurous passion is BASE jumping. She met her husband-to-be, John McEvoy, in the sport. If there is any other activity that puts the risks of mountaineering into perspective, it's BASE jumping. The risks are greater and the death rate is higher.

Sequoia and John embraced their shared passion for BASE jumping. Immersing herself in such a risky activity also helped provide Sequoia with a broader perspective into what motivated Marty to pursue mountaineering with such enthusiasm.

'I'm well aware that we're all human and we make decisions and sometimes certain things beyond our control can influence those decisions,' Sequoia explained. 'I think that I'm at peace with how Dad passed away. But I think it will probably take me the rest of my life to be at peace with my brother going too.'

Recently, Sequoia's husband John found out that he had a serious medical condition. 'For the last seven years, John has done the most dangerous sport in the world,' Sequoia said. 'And then he gets a brain tumour. Are you kidding me? If that doesn't show you that at any moment, you never know what's going to happen, then what on earth does? The irony of it is just insane to me.'

Sequoia explained that, despite the cancer, John wanted to

keep BASE jumping. 'If John were to stop jumping, a part of his soul would shrivel,' she said. 'The same thing applied to Dad. If he had ever stopped climbing, a part of his soul would shrivel. I would rather be with somebody whose soul is alive and well, even if they leave this earth too early, then have a long period of time with someone with a shrivelled soul.'

TWENTY-TWO

Meeting Sequoia after so many years, and then listening to her talk about her father and her attitude to life, illustrated an all-or-nothing approach to living and to taking risks. For Sequoia, it was a life that felt normal and right. No doubt, this quality and strength of character in Sequoia was, at least in part, passed on by the actions and beliefs of Marty.

Sequoia's views also helped me reflect further on my decision to stop climbing. And to question it. And to realise that I wanted to return to it. I needed to return to it.

It is better to live fully and passionately rather than half-live with regret. While I believe this attitude is desirable, if not essential, for everybody, it is certainly an attitude typical among risk-takers. It's also a convenient form of justification.

I'm not saying that this justification is wrong. I have used it in the past many times, both in my own mind and when talking to others. I understand that high levels of risk attract a certain personality type, someone who is able to commit. And commitment, stripped back to its bare necessity, is all or nothing. Make a decision, accept the consequences, whatever they may be, or else just ignore them, and then go for it.

There's another side to risk taking, especially around mountaineering, that I haven't focused on so far. I believe it is essential to acknowledge what happens at the bottom of the cliff, the place where the ambulance waits. Considering those who help us when we get into trouble adds perspective, or it should, to the consequences of our decision-making. For me, taking an opportunity to meet and spend time with a mountain rescue team should only help in my decision to return to climbing.

'Hurry up and wait' seems an appropriate mantra for any rescue team, and especially a full-time team. While most New Zealand search and rescue crews are made up of suitably skilled volunteers, the Aoraki / Mount Cook Alpine Rescue Team provides the country's only full-time, professional mountain rescue service. They are rightly considered the epitome of mountain rescue in this country.

Two teams of three responders with a floating fourth member alternate being on call for any emergencies throughout summer in the Aoraki / Mount Cook and Westland Tai Poutini National Parks and the surrounding mountainous areas. Supervisor Jono Gillan and team leaders Jim Young and Mark Evans have been employed all year by the Department of Conservation, and the other team members join them from October until April when the park is at its busiest.

The season I visited the team, to write about them for a magazine, the summer crew had an international feel. Lee Mackintosh, a rather strapping, self-confessed 'super keen climber' from the United Kingdom was into his third season, while Shane Rathbun from Northern California was starting his first. Vindy Hamilton and Khan Coleman, both in their twenties, managed to keep the home flag flying. Regardless of any cultural differences, there was plenty of friendly banter at the rescue base over coffee at morning briefings and during training scenarios.

Jono, who couldn't quite hide his own Australian twang, reckoned that the key to a top rate SAR team was to find and mesh the right blend of skills, experience, and personalities. 'There are some really strong rescuers in volunteer teams around the country,' he explained. 'Some of them are super experienced and have all the right qualifications.'

The difference between the Mount Cook team and other rescue teams, Jono pointed out, was the ability to be together all the time, and therefore become more practised in current rescue techniques.

'We're not having to rely on a large pool of volunteers with varied experience levels. It's a small team and the guys train together all the time. I encourage them to do as much climbing as possible so they are always up-skilling and familiar with each other. Regardless of which team responds to an incident, I know that their approach is going to be consistent.'

Jono himself was a fully qualified mountain guide, with fifteen years experience ski patrolling and ten years volunteering with the Whakatipu Alpine Cliff Rescue Team, based out of Queenstown. He reckoned that consistency in rescue practices was key, and he saw achieving this long-term as one of his main goals as the AMCART Supervisor.

'The Mount Cook team has always been a good training ground for developing young mountaineers,' he said. 'But, what tends to happen is guys either burn out after a couple of seasons or use the role as a stepping stone to something else. Moving forward, I want this to be an attractive job for high-end mountain professionals and for them to remain for more than just a couple of years.'

When the sun is overhead, and ominous-looking UFO-shaped clouds are nowhere to be seen, the grandest sight of Aoraki / Mount Cook draws camera-carrying tourists and summit-driven mountaineers like bees to a flower. But the hypnotic view and the motivation to walk further or climb higher can also be an unpredictable and sometimes dangerous precursor.

Being a mountain environment, there is a very defined edge to how far the inexperienced can safely venture. The popular Hooker Valley Track is a classic example. In the height of summer, thousands of tourists complete the two-to-four-hour round trip every day, pausing to take photos of themselves in front of the Hooker terminal lake and with Aoraki / Mount Cook and Mount Hicks dominating the skyline behind them.

As Mark Evans accurately observed, the popularity of selfie photos sees some people venturing just that bit further to capture an even more dramatic shot. And this also applies to the other end of the spectrum, with climbers high up in the mountains, in a much more dangerous environment.

'There's been a massive increase in those wanting to get first ascents or first ski descents or focus on key areas for selfies, geo tracking, you name it,' Mark said to me. 'It's not about the summit anymore. Rather, it's the need for an Instagram shot. And many of these people are lacking the necessary skills to make the right risk assessment of the conditions around them.'

Climate change is also having a dramatic effect, both on conditions in the park and on user habits. Shrinking glaciers make access to the higher, more popular peaks like Aoraki / Mount Cook and Mount Tasman increasingly difficult, and this means the peak climbing season is shifting from summer and squeezing into the more unstable weather conditions of spring.

When something goes wrong the emergency callout generally comes to AMCART from either the Police or the Rescue Coordination Centre New Zealand. The team leader and incident management team on standby assemble at the rescue centre as quickly as possible. First, the team ascertains the nature of the response required, be it to a climbing fall or an avalanche or someone who has been reported as overdue.

Jono explained that transport was a main consideration in working out how to respond to any rescue situation, and that the choice depended largely on the weather.

'How we can get to them is key. We quickly decide whether to use a helicopter or mount a terrestrial response,' he said. 'For a speedy response, a helicopter and longline rescue is vital.'

Usually, one or two rescuers will first complete a flyby of a site with the pilot to assess conditions, and then come in on the longline to secure the patient in either a lifting bridle or a stretcher.

'Speed but safety is always paramount,' said Jono, 'along with a bloody good pilot of course. We rely on them one hundred percent to keep us safe in what can be pretty testing flying conditions.'

The previous season had been a tough one for the team, with seven climbing fatalities in the park and a number of other challenging rescue and recovery operations. It was twenty-six-year-old Khan Coleman's first season with AMCART. Originally from the Hawkes Bay, Khan's outdoor experience was through ski patrolling on Mount Ruapehu and then two seasons glacier guiding on the Franz Josef Glacier.

'For sure, some rescues can be tougher than others,' he said to me. 'Especially if someone has fallen a long way. Personally, I try to take something positive from it. Learn from what has gone wrong rather than just focus on the negative side.'

Khan added that an important part of de-stressing after a tough scenario was to take the SAR gear off and be anonymous for a while.

'Quite often we go out as a team afterwards. We can talk openly with teammates or friends and family. And knowing that, if you are struggling a bit, it's not unusual. If I feel rattled, it's okay to take some time out.'

Mark agreed. 'It's not just about focussing on the loss of life. If we can help recover a body, there's a positive in that. They weren't lost to the mountains. We are the hope for the family, providing them with the opportunity for closure in dealing with the loss of their loved ones. A job like this can open your eyes, but I like to use that in a positive way.'

The AMCART team and I boarded a helicopter for a flight to Plateau Hut. I had been invited to join their training day as a rescue patient and also to experience first-hand how they operated in the mountains. I hadn't been to Plateau Hut since 1994, which was also the first and only time I climbed our highest, most revered maunga. As the helicopter hovered for landing close to the hut, situated on a rocky knoll overlooking the Grand Plateau, I glanced out the window. On the other side of the glacier, Aoraki / Mount Cook's east face rose in one clean, shimmering, shield of ice and snow.

I remembered looking down from the top of that face all those years ago, an absolute greenhorn climber attached by rope to another who wasn't much more experienced, both of us trying to work out what this alien alpine world was all about and how to stay safe in it. There were others up there seemingly as naive as us. A few climbers were even wandering through the broken icefall of the upper Linda Shelf unroped, and then for some inexplicable reason, a foreign pair decided to cross over our rope as both teams were pitching through the summit rocks. If somebody fell, everyone was going with them. Getting through that was lucky.

I also remembered some of the other climbers staying at Plateau Hut. There was an Australian, Duncan Chessell; he went on to climb the seven highest summits in each of the world's seven continents. Duncan is one of the few Australian mountaineers to have climbed and guided Mount Everest and the first South Australian to summit. He has summited Everest three times, in 2001, 2007, and 2010.

There was also another Australian, Andrew McAuley, who later became a renowned mountaineer and sea kayaker. McAuley's second attempt at paddling from Australia to New Zealand began on 11 January 2007. It ended a month later, when the search for his missing body was called off after the recovery of his partly-flooded kayak about fifty kilometres short of his designated landing point at Milford Sound.

Kiwi Anton Wopereis was also staying at Plateau Hut while guiding a client on Aoraki / Mount Cook. He was a knowledgeable, and very welcome, source of information for my climbing partner Grant and me on our own climbs of Mount Dixon and Aoraki. Years later, Anton fell and died while climbing in the summer of 2009. He had been attempting his thirty-first summit of Aoraki, and was guiding another client.

Seeing the mountain again up close and remembering my past experience there made me realise how much that experience, along with other experiences on other mountains, meant to me. I felt connected to the mountaineering culture. It was an environment that I understood.

On this day, after Jono got me to tie in to the other end of his rope, we wandered easily up snow slopes to a ridge leading towards Mount Dixon. First up for the team training was practising helicopter drop-offs and pick-ups. Jono and I watched as Mark explained to the others the finer points of longline rescues, with the picturesque sweep of the Tasman Glacier curving away in the background.

From this angle, I couldn't quite see Mount Walter farther up the glacier, where I had great memories of climbing a few years earlier with Jamie, Shelley, and Kester. This was a magical part of the country. I wondered to myself why it had taken so long to return here.

Later, we moved down to a crevassed area of the Grand Plateau. This was where I got to experience my first 'rescue'. Needless to point out, it was a little unsettling being placed in a stretcher and then lowered out over the abyss of a crevasse (as a climber I am used to having control over my own ropework and anchors). But there was nothing I could do other than lie back, dodge bits of falling ice from the overhanging edge of the crevasse, admire the professionals at work, and be thankful that this wasn't for real.

Spending time with AMCART was a great experience. It certainly allowed me to reconsider my own motivations and decision-making around climbing, and then understand them in a more holistic way. Knowing that my conservative approach to risk wasn't uncommon, helped confirm that returning to climbing—if and when I was ready—was the right decision.

TWENTY-THREE

The Dasler Pinnacles are one of the more prominent and popular mountains to climb in the Hopkins Valley. From the valley floor, the twin summits might appear rather intimidating. Two spikes tower above the bush line, seemingly protected by steep rocky ridges on every side, and a western aspect split by a deep gash—an almost right-angled fold through the rock's strata into the heart of the mountain.

A number of routes, both rock and ice, lead up through the varied terrain on this side of the mountain. Yet it is one of the easier routes—the North ridge—that is possibly the best to experience.

From the valley floor, a steep track heads up through the beech forest towards the Pinnacles, reaching the rather cramped Dasler Bivouac after an hour or so of heavy sweating. You can either spend the night at the hut or carry on up a faint track through alpine shrubbery, weaving between occasional rock outcrops, to camp on a flattish grassy terrace right at the very base of the rock slabs leading up the west face. In the past, I have managed to find a small trickle of water every time I bivvied there.

The North ridge, which I have climbed with others and on my own on numerous occasions, is a pleasant, if somewhat exposed, scramble on good quality rock. The route finishes directly at a summit with perhaps the finest viewpoint in the valley. While in winter, runnels of ice and frozen snow change the nature of the mountain considerably, in summer it is a perfect place to ease back into the feeling of exposure.

Jamie and I ventured here many times over the years. On one trip that sticks in my mind, we came to look at a route on a face of another mountain near to Dasler Pinnacles that I had ogled for a number of years. But the snowpack had been twitchy, and the weather was deteriorating. Jamie gave in easily when I suggested a different, safer, option.

We found a thin streak of ice on the lower western wall of Dasler Pinnacles, almost like a lightning strike up the rock, and that had enough spice in its pitches to keep the both of us satisfied. I remember walking back down the valley with my friend, the snow falling lightly across the landscape, and the both of us laughing at how lucky we had been to squeeze a climb in before the storm hit.

Talking to Sequoia, and then to Jono and the other members of AMCART, had certainly helped put my thoughts into perspective. I guess my supposedly being finished with climbing was more of an extended leave of absence. In part, it had been so I could process my grief over the loss of Jamie and Marty, as well as how it affected my own decision-making in the mountains. It shouldn't come as a surprise that climbing accidents place stress on climbers, their loved ones, and the services tasked with rescuing, or recovering, them. I had been down this road before, and understood that I possibly would be again.

My withdrawn state of mind was making sense. But it felt like I could still do with a different perspective, perhaps a more moderate perspective. The way back to climbing should be familiar. Small steps.

My friend and work colleague David 'Stretch' Newstead also returned to mountaineering as a middle-aged man, as well as a father with responsibilities. With a background in hard rock climbing, David had only done sporadic trips into the mountains over the years.

David seemed an ideal partner to tackle a rock route on the West face of the Daslers. He has an easy-going attitude and an infectious enthusiasm for the freedom of just being able to go climbing in a beautiful environment. I knew that it wouldn't matter to him whether we actually climbed anything or not.

We left my vehicle and started to walk up the valley. David threw his pack on and headed off at a great rate—sheer enthusiasm for what lay ahead drove him, he told me later. Given my current, more moderate state of fitness, I decided against trying to keep up. Instead, I paced myself in the knowledge of the height gain to come. I caught David about halfway up the steep, forested track leading to Dasler Bivouac, at the point where a permanently-fixed rope is required to surmount a short section of slabby rock.

He was puffing, red-faced from exertion, and in need of a rest. I laughed, before slowly continuing on past him.

'See you at the hut for a cuppa,' I said, trying to hide a grin.

Given my recent musings, I was interested to get David's

take on what it was about climbing that appealed to him. So, at our bivouac on the flat grassy slope at the base of the West face the night before the climb—once he'd finally arrived and recovered from the exertion—I asked what had attracted him to climbing.

'Perhaps it was the memory of a Wednesday evening as a youngster watching a television episode of *That's Incredible*,' David said. 'I remember a shirtless, blond-haired climber hanging rope-less from the tips of his fingers at the lip of a huge limestone overhang in France.'

Many years later, my friend saw the clip again. This time he recognised the climber as Patrick Edlinger (or 'Edgeclinger', as he was affectionally known). 'Le Blond', was one of the early sport-climbing Gods that had created an impression on David in his preteens.

'His seemed the ultimate expression of freedom and self-reliance,' David explained. 'Even then, I think I recognised it as something that was more than just being reckless and irresponsible.'

Like me, David also recalled the unexplained urge to climb trees in his youth—to want to go up.

'We had a 100-foot high macrocarpa hedge that I used to chase one of our pet possums up. Far too high for my parents' liking, I'm sure. But just high enough to be aware of the consequences and measuring each branch's weight-holding ability a little more carefully.'

There we were, many decades from our youth, at the base of what we took for a macrocarpa hedge these days. The freedom of self-reliance was still present, as was the urge to climb.

'My climbing seems to have settled into somewhat of a happy middle-aged place,' David said to me. 'As much as I have enjoyed the physical challenge of it all, I've always experienced it as a personal, internal challenge. Overcoming my own fears rather than beating someone else. Grades and difficulty are important but not as much as the mere pleasure of moving over rock.'

David reflected that time had mellowed his attitude to climbing. 'I have watched younger friends drop away from the sport as their life happened,' he said. 'But I keep feeling the need to return to it, like an old comfy jersey. Even while dabbling in other pursuits, whatever they might be, climbing always feels right. Familiar. Comfortable. Pleasurable.'

David's thinking helped reinforce my own, and especially how I was now slowly edging my way back into it. His motivation to climb seemed considered rather than all-encompassing. And, because of this, his attitude to risk taking felt more balanced and in sync with my own.

The next morning was clear and sunny, and we took our time sipping coffee and looking up at the angles and slabs on the West face of Daslers. We searched for a line that appealed to us. I spotted a clean-looking, left-slanting slab that led to what seemed like a steeper, and more challenging, arête. Not knowing, or particularly caring, whether it had been climbed before, the potential route seemed as good an option as anything else on the face. Yes, I was nervous at the start, but I felt comfortable in David's company and attitude. This seemed right.

David offered to lead the first pitch. But, for a change, I felt determined to tackle my doubts head on. I smiled, and took the rope from his hands. Ironically, there was absolutely no protection for the entire rope length until I found a suitable belay. *Welcome back to climbing!*

The sun continued to shine, and we cruised up the warmed

rock. There was a short section of crumbly, difficult climbing. As luck would have it, that was David's lead! I enjoyed the front row seat, of watching someone confident in their ability on challenging terrain. David moved with grace.

Reaching the summit ridge later in the day, I felt as good about climbing and myself as I had for a long time. My decision to return had provided me with a sense of relief. I had been burdening myself by choosing not to climb. Here, I wasn't doing damage to the memories of Jamie and Marty. I was extending the experiences that I had shared with them. Here, I was honouring them.

David had been a great climbing partner—competent, conscientious, and positive. He was certainly someone I could go on and try something more committing with in the future. My mind wandered through possibilities. *The search begins again.*

We sat on the summit for as long as time allowed, enjoying the sun's warmth and the ambience of being up high. The valley stretched away beneath our feet, and other mountains filled the horizon in all directions. Many of these mountains I knew well, like remembering past experiences while looking at photos in an album. It felt a privilege to know an environment such as this so intimately and profoundly.

David was leaning back against the rock with his eyes closed, like a lizard sunning itself. David's face had a contemplative look. Then he opened his eyes. He took in the view again, before speaking.

'Climbing is such a qualitative pursuit,' he said. 'Everyone's experience and motivations in the sport are different and equally valid. While I understand, and sometimes find myself jealous of those motivated purely by chasing grades, I've never found that overly motivating. I just want to climb.'

TWENTY-FOUR

The author Joan Didion was once quoted as saying: 'I don't write for catharsis. I have to write to understand.'

This book has been as much about me understanding how to come to terms with loss as it is about understanding why I choose to climb. Just as life can be considered a journey, with its ups and downs, its joyous times and its unknowns, so is a mountaineering trip a microcosm of that journey. We conceive a goal, and then make the best plans we can to reach that goal. We allow for variables. We deal with the risk. We accept the chance of failure. We try to have fun, and most of the time we succeed in doing so.

Sometimes, I have to remind myself of this. If, and when, I focus too much on the consequence of risk and then loss and the burden on making the right decisions and on those left behind, I find myself losing perspective. Talking to Sequoia, and David, and the guys at AMCART has helped to re-establish that. After all, a life without risk is, really, no life at all.

A friend Kynan Bazley once said to me, 'The dignity of risk should be afforded to everyone.' It was the winter of 2004, and North Elcho's confined alpine valley had piled high with avalanche debris. Having picked the least exposed site we could find to pitch our tent, Kynan and I zipped up into our cosy sleeping bags beneath a cirque of snowy slopes and settled in for a long, cold evening. Mount Ward's steep and icy southeast face—the feature we'd come to climb—faded with the light, but still played with our psyche.

I remember lying there and being struck by Kynan's choice of words. They also helped to take my mind off what waited for us the following day. My friend went on to add that, too often, we are denied the opportunity to take risk because of societal judgements and laws. 'If I decide to climb a mountain,' he said, 'my decision reflects how I see the world and where I fit into it. Risk is an important part of that.'

Although this was something I agreed with, I decided to play devil's advocate. 'That's fine, but climbing is not essential like driving a car, is it?' I replied.

'We as humans have needs,' Kynan countered, probably realising I was leading him on but enjoying the gist of the conversation. 'I believe self-actualisation comes at the top. We should be more inclined to take risks to feel good about ourselves rather than in the mundane day-to-day stuff.'

Since that cold night, I've found myself reflecting on Kynan's 'dignity of risk' comment many times. I find it all the more profound given that, as a doctor, his daily job is to save lives. Some people would consider this being in direct conflict with Kynan completing a number of bold mountain climbs around the world, climbs where he has risked both his own life and the lives of his willing climbing partners. But Kynan, and indeed most who participate in outdoor adventure activities, don't see it that way.

That's fine. Adventurous activity isn't for everyone. And if I didn't climb, I'd miss it. I'd miss the way it made me feel before, during, and afterwards. I also believe I would feel less complete without it.

So, really, my so-called angst is little more than a decision-making process. Like Will Gadd's 'positive power of negative thinking', I use it in a way that works for me. The ongoing navel-gazing about 'what if' is healthy as long as I channel it the right way. I still need to remind myself to let go.

The Danish philosopher and poet Soren Kierkegaard once wrote, 'The highest and most beautiful things in life are not to be heard about, or read about, nor seen but, if one will, are to be lived.'

What do I take from this? *Don't think so much, Paul. Just get on with it.*

But then Kierkegaard also wrote that 'Life can only be understood backwards, but it must be lived forwards'.

There's an obvious dichotomy here. Conscious—conscientious—decisions around risk require understanding. The best way to understand is to learn from experience, from what has gone before. Yes, get on with it, but not at all costs all the time. And, so, I try to hedge my bets.

There's one more quote on this topic that I'd like to share, one that probably captures my feelings best, especially when it comes to thinking about Jamie and Marty. It's a line by the actor Morgan Freeman from one of my favourite movies, *The Shawshank Redemption*: '...the place you live in is that much more drab and empty now that they're gone. I guess I just miss my friend(s).'

I miss my friends. Climbing in the mountains is an attempt to make my life less drab and empty. It is also a reminder of Marty and Jamie and others, and a fitting memorial to them.

TWENTY-FIVE

The Darran Mountains lie deep in the marrow of northern Fiordland. A chunky, perplexing range of diorites and sandstones, gneisses and granites, this is a land of extremes, with the country's most remote summits, the greatest rainfall and the longest, hardest-to-climb alpine rock walls. Adventurers have been coming here since William Grave and Arthur Talbot in the late 1800s, to test themselves against the climate and forge new routes in what is still largely an untapped, vertical landscape.

'It is in the Darrans that we are most directly confronted with the reality of our limits,' wrote climber Tom Hoyle in *Vertical Life* magazine.

This quote sums up why these special mountains have called to me and to many other modern-day climbers. I find myself drawn forward—upward—perhaps first by a gentle curve of frozen snow, and then the sharpening edge of a buttress of rock that might rise for hundreds of metres. The challenge is both in front of me and within me, trying to manage the delicate balance between the challenging landscape, the changeable weather, and the potential for risk and reward.

As a range of mountains, the peaks of the Darrans aren't that high or spread out. There are around eighty recognised summits in an area less than sixty kilometres long and twenty-five kilometres wide, bordered to the east by the straight-armed sweep of the Hollyford Valley and the cold dark shadows of the Tasman Sea to the west. At 2723 metres, the highest is Mount Tūtoko, with the second-highest, Mount Madeline (2536 metres), nestled in its shadow.

Further east and northeast, the Southern Alps act as a 500-kilometre barrier along the spine of the South Island. Moist clouds, rolling in from the ocean, collide against their western flanks. In the Darrans, this phenomenon can mean an annual rainfall in excess of seven metres!

Despite their relatively small geographical area, the Darrans are renowned as a world-class climbing destination, rising sharply from the lowlands—castles of stone and ice, with sheer rock walls guarding their flanks. This area of Fiordland is bush choked and fjord chiselled. Few tracks pierce the 8000 square kilometres of austere, rain-drenched, mountainous country. Smoothed surfaces of dark glacial lakes reflect a land that's difficult to penetrate, where swift-running rivers cut through steep-sided valleys, and thickset forests remain untroubled by the few who manage to pass beneath them.

The only road access is from the small town of Te Anau, the Milford Highway, which tracks the eastern edge of Lake Te Anau before penetrating the flanks of the Southern Alps. Mountains approach from the west, gently at first with bush skirts and sloping ridges. But, pass over The Divide, and the mood of the landscape changes markedly.

Early explorers followed this narrowing valley beside the upper torrent of the Hollyford River, until they were met with what seemed to be impassable rock. The physical presence of walls more than a kilometre high, only a few hundred metres from today's highway, is still a breath-taking sight. The mountains here can appear humbling, if not disturbing, offering potential for routes that climbers dream and, perhaps, have nightmares about.

William Grave was one of the first to make tentative forays up these colossal fortresses in the late 1800s, following discontinuous chinks in their defences. Grave was a North Otago schoolteacher who, during his annual holidays, felt an 'irresistible impulse' to venture into what he described as the 'fastnesses of nature'.

For years, Grave and another adventurer, Arthur Talbot, searched for a route from near the source of the Hollyford River, over Homer Saddle, west into Cleddau Valley, and finally arriving at the already-popular tourist resort at Milford Sound. Until that time, visitors to the sound could only reach it by boat, but the New Zealand Government was keen for access through the mountains to bolster tourism.

Finally, in 1909, after several attempts, Grave and Talbot discovered a route that would become known as Talbot's Ladder—a precarious, unlikely spur above Homer Saddle that led towards Mount McPherson. With dizzying airspace on both sides, this was probably the first significant rock route climbed in the Darrans. Reaching a peak they called 'the Snowball' (Mount McPherson) the men were still faced with a traverse northwest along a ridge towards Mount Isolation, and then a slippery descent below Grave/Talbot Pass along grassy dead-end ledges, and finally down to the Esperance River and the Cleddau Valley. While not at all suitable as a tourist trail, rather astoundingly, this became a recognised mail route into the sound.

Just over a century later, the Darran Mountains have become home to New Zealand's most technical climbs, both in summer on the huge rock walls, and in winter when the walls become frozen sheets of ice. While little may have changed since the days of Grave and Talbot in terms of access, better weather forecasting allows the modern-day climber a greater chance of success.

And yet, the mountains remain just as challenging. For the climber, there's little opportunity for direct assault; one must scurry, mouse-like, up frightening terraces festooned with slippery mosses and grasses; sneak along broken shelves stubbled with hebes; and baulk at ledges that end abruptly mid-wall as often as not, all just to get to the real climbing. It's this unique combination of elements that creates a sense of intricacy—and urgency—in trips here, for there are endlessly varied combinations and always new spaces to explore.

I came to the Darrans with a small team of climbers to follow in the pioneering footsteps of Grave and Talbot, and to test our own limits on unclimbed walls in the range. We would discover soon enough why they had remained unclimbed for so long.

I was also here for another reason. My passion for climbing had been reignited, but I needed to build on it. Gently. With care.

David Newstead passed his fingers across a slab of mottled granite, searching for weakness—a divot, an edge, a knob of rock. But the bald granite face offered little purchase. The ropes tied to him remained untethered, falling in a long arc back to our belay. If he slipped, he would drop four stories to the glacier below.

David and I had tramped to this remote location near the head of Moraine Creek. Above us, the summits of Apirana Peak and Mount Revelation curved towards a sky clear of cloud, the unclimbed wall we were attempting squeezed between them like a rumple in the landscape. With an unnamed high point at over 1700 metres, we had been attracted by the look of clean, sun-bleached granite and the promise of a challenging climb. A narrow glacier allowed us to crampon up the shadows partway beneath its face.

Attached to David's harness was an assortment of nuts, camming devices, and pitons, all designed to be placed in cracks in the rock and then clipped to the ropes, offering some protection against a tumble into the void. But, none of them had been used.

Already, I had completed the first pitch above the glacier, a series of broken, angled ledges, leading up to the point where the wall steepened considerably; now my climbing companion was immersed in the intricacies of difficult route finding.

'Watch me,' he called, before attempting a series of moves that, from below, appeared ambitious. Twist and lock, reach, crimp, step high. David contorted his body into unusual positions, mirroring the rock, performing something resembling a vertical yoga: Sun Salutation, perhaps.

Below, at the belay, I held my breath. David completed the sequence, sidling towards relative safety in an easier-angled scoop. It was a small win, but above him, the featureless slab continued without a blemish. This route, it seemed, had remained unclimbed for a good reason.

David edged forwards a few more precious centimetres, his fingertips searching the steep slab before withdrawing. Without an anchor to reduce the risk, proceeding further would be madness. He managed a retreat, picking his way carefully down the rock wall the same way he came up.

This attempt was a defeat, but arching walls, buttresses, and arêtes surrounded us on all sides. Hectares of rock stretched to the skyline, offering a multitude of possibilities for a first ascent...and one, in particular, higher up the valley.

East Twin is one of a triplet of rock pyramids inland from Milford Sound. During Grave and Talbot's descent into the Esperance, no doubt they would have eyed the summits of East Twin, West Twin, and The Sentinel with amazement—from the valley floor, these alarmingly steep walls rise for almost a mile. These days, when viewed from the spectacular but easily-accessed Gertrude Saddle, tourists gape at the sudden exposure, the three summits framing a view that sweeps down into Milford Sound and the iconic Mitre Peak.

In attempting to climb one of these peaks, David and I were following the footsteps of some of this country's best—and most stubborn—climbers, including Lindsay Stewart, a Dunedin medical student who became entranced by the Darrans during the 1930s. Stewart, along with Jim Dakin and Jack Warren, made the first ascent of East Twin in 1936, along its southeast ridge. This remains one of only three new climbs on the mountain, its summit probably reached no more than a handful of times in the decades since Stewart's first ascent.

For our next (hopefully more successful) trip two weeks later, David and I were accompanied by Elke Braun-Elwert, a Tekapo based climber and guide. Elke had taken over her father's, Gottlieb Braun-Elwert's, guiding company, Alpine Recreation, becoming the first father/daughter mountain guides in the country. For Elke, this trip was an opportunity for some 'amateur' climbing before her final international level guiding assessment. Recalling that she had previously climbed with Marty, I was looking forward to finally doing a trip with her.

The three of us were aiming for the east face of East Twin, an unclimbed curve of rock that I had first spotted years earlier when exploring high above the dark water of Lake Adelaide, and then again studied during the recent trip up Moraine Creek with David. Steep, rising around 400 metres above a glacier at its highest point, the wall seemed to have plenty of features that should allow numerous climbing opportunities.

Looking up at a face like that has always filled me with a certain level of apprehension. Judging its true difficulty was impossible without committing to trying to climb it. But the appearance of the wall had me hooked and I vowed to return.

David, Elke, and I made our way past the last day trippers at Gertrude Saddle, and within minutes, found ourselves alone in a nearly vertical landscape, traversing narrow terraces under the summit of Barrier Knob, across a section of rock referred to by some as the 'sui-sidle'. While not difficult in climbing terms, the huge, exposed drop below the ledge and the slippery, wet lichen added to the risk and the atmosphere.

By evening, we had found smoothed slabs flat enough to spend the night on, the rock warmed by the last evening light.

As we prepared dinner, I thought it was a good time to ask Elke about her experiences climbing with Marty.

'What I really liked about Marty was that he saw the best in people even if they didn't see it in themselves,' she said. 'He had this amazing ability to get people to realise their own potential, not in a pushy way, but with boundless energy and encouragement. He would be, "How can we make this work".'

Elke's comments made me smile, and then also remember Marty's encouragement towards my own climbing goals. Sitting in this beautiful part of New Zealand, and with a potentially huge challenge waiting for us tomorrow, this seemed a perfect place to reflect on how much he had influenced my life.

'Marty could get people to express their dreams, and then go about encouraging them to make it happen,' Elke continued. 'He would just get those who trusted him to be able to achieve something far greater than they ever thought possible. Not many people have that skill.'

As twilight came, and we settled into our bivouac bags, I couldn't help but think more of Marty, and then Jamie, and then also of who else may have passed by this way, perhaps spending the night in the same spot and looking out over the same mountain summits.

Nearly two decades after Lindsay Stewart's climbing in the 1930s, another Dunedin medical student pored obsessively through the pages of Stewart's written adventures.

'As I reread his account of those climbs,' wrote Mike Gill in his book *Mountain Midsummer*, 'I seemed to find the same enthusiasm (as Stewart) and sense of wonder...the same awareness of the magic of the landscape, the same zeal for exploring its landmarks and byways.'

Gill was staying in the same Dunedin hostel during his 1956 medical studies as the young Phil Houghton when he noticed that a new ice axe had been delivered to Houghton's room. Gill poked his head through the doorway. 'See you do a bit of climbing,' he said. 'I do a bit myself.'

Gill later described Houghton's car as a 'poor maltreated Morris Minor called Doodle whose scarlet and cream paintwork showed dimly through dust accumulated on backcountry roads...On the back seat and in boot there was always a litter of primuses, old food, plastic bags, pitons, fragments of rope, and sometimes a dead rabbit.'

Gill and Houghton went on to complete a number of first ascents in the area, including the west ridge of Sabre Peak in 1959, an impressive fin of rock that I could see from my bivvy site with David and Elke, its skyline ridges silhouetted by the setting sun. Regardless of tomorrow's outcome, I already felt a part of the landscape and its history.

Here stretched a library of mountains, spine after spine silhouetted against a gently warming sky of azure and mauve. In this half-light before dawn, shelves of open-faced granite rose before me, weathered and sun-bleached. One aspect of the rock appeared intriguing, like the blank pages of a book. The very first page.

We were starting the first pitch on the east face of East Twin, deciding to attempt a steep slab that angled up and right, split by ledges and overhangs which we would hopefully be able to traverse around.

Unclimbed and subtly featured, the wall hinted at a passage, the vague possibility of holds, perhaps the faintest of cracks here and there, which I had studied intently from below before choosing to commit. *Are they deep enough to take a nestled wire? A small cam? Offering up enough security to lure me upwards?*

I retightened my harness and fondled my rope like a loved pet. Always, it seems, the essence of climbing waits just beyond that point where we think the limit for our ability exists. *Yes, this is where I would like the next chapter of my story to begin.*

The sun's first rays danced across the wall, flashes of white light in my eyes and my mind. The rays were like pages from the book being flicked quickly through, one after the other by a gust of wind, forwards or backwards. I couldn't tell.

Blinking my eyes against the sudden glare, I tried to clear my mind. *Breathe. Focus.*

I started tentatively, like always, rubbing the tips of my fingers against cold stone to acknowledge its presence, dipping them into my chalk bag, and then blowing gently across them like I'd done so many times that it wasn't even a conscious decision anymore. I placed the toe of my shoe against a shallow divot to test friction, squinted my eyes in concentration, and then took another deep, noise-cleansing breath.

A tongue of glacial ice arched overhead to my right. It shadowed the rock, droplets leaving dark water streaks across patches of lichen.

Elke pointed at the wet slab beneath the ice. 'Perhaps there might be easier,' she suggested quietly. 'A bit more featured, don't you think?'

But I was having none of it. In a world of friction, damp is like lubricant. 'Thanks. But that looks pretty slippery. I reckon I'll have a go further to the left.'

Where I had chosen to start appeared to be a bit harder. Quite hard, actually, but surely it wouldn't be too bad.

I stepped off the ground. *Up, always up*, I told myself. My toe placated the divot. My fingers fondled this hardened slab of the earth's bedrock that had been thrust skywards, twisted and faulted, rasped smooth by glaciers long since melted to the sea. There was a harsh warning screech off somewhere in the sky, a kea, perhaps offering what it thought was sage advice.

Instead, I chose to focus on David's soothing words, echoing faintly in the alcove as he belayed. It didn't matter what he said, just the knowledge he was there and his tone comforting.

'Looking good, Paul. Yep, I reckon that crack up there could take some gear. Definitely...No? Well, maybe the one a bit higher and to your left. Keep going mate. Keep moving up. It'll be fine. Just a bit more.'

There I was, perched on a grey and mottled wall, feeling for its mood, studying enticing ripples that stretched across the page, waiting to be filled with my words and sentences, a story told with my body and from within my mind.

I kept climbing in the direction David had indicated. There were no real holds, but enough friction allowed me to apply a second's pressure and then move on. The first crack in the rock was a few metres up, but it wasn't deep enough to place any protection. The next crack was even worse. I paused and glanced down. Just for a moment. *Nope, no going back that way.* At least I wouldn't die if I fell, not immediately anyway.

I edged upwards for a few more precious moves, more cautious now, my fingertips performing another search of the steep slab before withdrawing. Then I glanced down again, looking straight at Dave. He said nothing, but I could read the doubt on his face, which meant he could certainly read it on mine. The voice inside my head started to scream: *There is no fucking gear!*

My mind raced itself in a search for options. Higher up appeared to offer the same protection-less blankness. If I carried on, I'd be soloing up most of the pitch. The climbing looked hard. One slip and...

Maybe if I jump out far enough, I'll clear the rock and land on the glacier, sliding safely down soft snow.

The thought hovered as an option for far too long.

I couldn't go up. I couldn't go down. My fingertips were tiring, and my calves beginning to tighten from holding this stance too long. My story was becoming lost in a jumble of rushed words, none of them making sense anymore.

There was a grovelly-looking corner crack way out left that I told myself I could probably—maybe—reach. But then I'd be committed to doing crack moves, which I normally tried to avoid. I hate climbing cracks. They feel so devoid of finesse. Rather than moving smoothly from hold to hold, they require an uncomfortable thrutching technique.

Somehow, something happened in that grovelly-looking corner that instantly blanked itself from my mind (even now I can't recall what I did in there). The next thing I knew, I was a pathetic heap back at the base of the climb, slumped on a small stack of boulders next to David and Elke, complaining of a strained ego-flexor and swearing myself off trying to do any more new alpine rock routes altogether.

I could tell that my display had also put David off. He said nothing, looking with a far-away focus out over the gentle curve of the lake and valley below us.

It was then that Elke stepped forward and asked if she could give it a shot. I untied the ropes from my harness and handed them over.

A few minutes and moves later, Elke called down: 'Pass me the hammer.'

'What?'

'The hammer. Pass it up.'

David and I glanced at each other. On first consideration,

using an ice hammer to climb rock in the height of summer seemed rather unorthodox. But, I handed the tool to our friend without mentioning this small detail.

Elke stepped tentatively up, onto a thin wedge in the rock. She steadied herself, swung and thunked the hammer into the rotten, overhanging ice, gripping it with one hand while smearing her climbing shoes up the wet, smoothed, almost featureless slab.

I found myself holding my breath. To the surprise of both of us on the ground, the pick of the hammer and Elke's shoes remained firmly placed. She leaned in towards the rock, balancing carefully on the thinnest of slivers so she could remove the hammer, and then imbed it into the ice further up. She sneaked up again. *This might actually work.*

Minutes ticked by. A light breeze brushed across the face. The kea called out again, sounding like it had found a rocky perch on the ridge above us. By now, Elke had manoeuvred herself to a stance past the tongue of ice where the rock became more featured. She clipped the hammer to her harness and, just before disappearing around a corner, looked down and gave us a thumbs up and a huge grin.

Where I failed, Elke had taken up the narrative. My story became her story.

'Great idea, Elke,' I called up. 'Awesome climbing.' And then, quietly to David, quite possibly in a tone of voice that suggested a mix of admiration and self-motivating jealousy: 'Why didn't I think of that?'

Elke disappeared over a prow of rock, and the twin ropes slithered quietly after her, the only indication we had that she was continuing to make progress. Sixty metres above us—the length of the ropes—and some time later, she called out, 'Safe.' With early morning sun finally starting to warm the face, it was our turn to climb.

The sky was free of cloud, the air almost still. As I started the climb, rather than being weighted by the increasing airspace below, I focused on what was in front of me: small details on the rock that allowed me to move, the quiet concentration required of me, the way the chalk felt against coarse granite, the clink of karabiners on my harness as I dislodged a wire from the crack it had been wedged into, the careful breathing and focus that keep me in the here and the now. I was so focused on climbing that it came as a surprise to reach the broad ledge Elke was belaying from.

A nasty-looking overhang reared across the wall above us. It was David's turn to lead, and he carefully racked the karabiners and wires and cams on his harness, within easy reach for when he might need them.

'Maybe out to the right,' I suggested, indicating a steep but well-featured shorter wall that looked like it traversed across and around the difficulties. But we could only see for a few metres, the rest of the climb refusing to reveal itself from this position. David nodded without replying and started to climb.

David's pitch and every pitch thereafter was challenging, the positioning and choice of anchors a unique puzzle to solve. But every solution found encouraged the lead climber enough to carry on up the next arête and around the next corner.

With climbing, the higher you rise, the higher the stakes become, and the harder it is to pack it all in and turn back if the moves suddenly become too difficult. But these are the acute balances to strike, whether to keep climbing up or to turn around. Attempting a new route in a place such as this, any misjudgements can be costly.

Waiting at a belay, I looked out over the glacier and Lake

Adelaide, hundreds of metres below us now, smiling to myself despite the challenges that remained, hoping that my love for this experience, and this landscape of ours, would never diminish.

The last lead was again David's, a final apex of rock that would place us high on the summit ridge of East Twin. Finally, the climbing was a little bit easier, and we felt relaxed. We knew we would reach the top. The wind increased. Clouds drifted by. Another hour passed, and Elke and I followed. Then there was nothing more to climb.

Where we stood would have likely only been reached by a handful of others before us. And we had found a new route to get there, a line that was both stimulating and rewarding.

And yet, the route was only half completed. Often, the most challenging, and sometimes most dangerous, part of climbing a mountain is the getting off it again. The sun was well on its way towards the western horizon and on every side of us, steep drops disappeared into the void. The only means to descend was by abseil, back down the same way we had climbed.

The ice hammer was produced again, this time to be used in a more orthodox manner, whacking pitons into cracks in the rock so we had secure anchors to abseil from. Being the heaviest, I got the role of going first to test the security of each anchor placement.

Sometime later, back on a flattish knob of rock at the start of the route, I watched shadows lengthen across the wall we had climbed, and waited for the others to complete the final abseil. Behind me, hidden by the wall we had just succeed on, was Mitre Peak. In December 1955, Gill stood alone on its narrow, finlike summit and looked inland across an 'unknown array of ridges and ice falls and grey rock faces'.

For Gill, and generations of climbers who followed him—me included—falling in love with the mountains was like any other love. 'There comes a moment when you are aware of someone uniquely and bewitchingly different,' he wrote. 'I was smitten hopelessly.'

I wasn't smitten hopelessly, but I did feel a level of contentment in the mountains that I hadn't felt for a long time. It was almost peaceful in my mind. I accepted where I was and why. My body carried that level of fatigue that I craved and had been missing. My mind felt free of the need to judge.

Despite all of the angst and loss that climbing had caused me over the years, it was a relief to realise that I could still find fulfilment with moving up. I didn't have to push as hard as I had in the past; just being immersed in and challenged by the mountains provided enough satisfaction.

Not to say that this hadn't been a challenging climb, a tough climb with an unknown outcome right until we reached the top of the final pitch. There was nothing more to ascend. We had ascended it competently and as safely as possible. Part of me took pride in that we had tried to complete it in the best and safest style possible.

During the walk out, I took some time to think about Jamie and Marty and the positive influence they had on my life. Being in the mountains is when I feel their presence the most. It is a feeling that I cherish, and imagine will keep cherishing for as long as I am breathing.

TWENTY-SIX

The mountains of Ka Tiritiri O Te Moana draw the length of Te Waipounamu. From the East Coast they appear as a seemingly never-ending horizon, distant summits lifting to focus with first light. But travel closer and they become great cleaves of earth, their highest points guarded by dark ridges and cliffs without blemish.

During the winter months, snow smothers their flanks. Over time, the snow compresses into tongues of ice that slide with gravity and the weight of more snow from above. Or the snow may release in an instant, a bond somehow lost within the myriad of intricacies of the crystals.

In summer, the snow melts. Scree inclines carry to the valleys. Eastern plains of this alpine detritus extend as far as the eye can see, stirred by the hot, dry northwesters and braided by rivers of glacial thaw. These plains continue beyond the coast, a gradual conveyer of the long-forgotten summits now hidden beneath the Pacific Ocean.

In Central Otago, Lake Whakatipu carves a bolt of liquid lightning through the mountains. Never more than five kilometres wide, its glacial-fed water stretches eighty kilometres from Glenorchy in the north, doglegging past the tourist resort of Queenstown, to Kingston in the south.

Filtering into the lake's northernmost reach, the Dart River has flowed from the heart of the Southern Alps. Whakatipu is New Zealand's longest lake. The deepest point is sixty metres below sea level.

Overlooking Queenstown and Lake Whakatipu is the Remarkables Mountain Range. Easily accessed by one road, which leads up to a ski field with the same name, these mountains are a magnet for adventurers and tourists who want to stretch their legs during the summer months, and the hordes of snow enthusiasts when the mountains are blanketed by white in winter. There are a range of routes to climb, varying in grade from the easy to the particularly testing, and both during summer and winter. For me, the Remarkables are also a place to remember.

Writing can be cathartic. After Jamie died, his partner Jess started writing to help express what she was feeling, and to try to cope with her loss. I found one of her passages particularly moving:

'It's funny that when someone dies, everyone claims they couldn't say a bad word about the person. Most of the time this is a complete lie. I would say that in relation to Jamie this is almost true. But I will let you in on a secret. He was supremely confident. As supremely confident as they come. He was adamant that he had it all figured out, knew more than the next person and was the ultimate human; in health, behaviour, integrity, character, and love. As far as I am concerned he was the ultimate human and this was reflected in the incredible life he was living.

'Let me share a few other of Jamie's loves. The things he didn't write about but that were just as important to him as climbing. There was bread. His obsession for bread had been steadily growing. He thought about it, talked about it, made it, ate it, shared it, and loved it. Only two days after Mahe was born, he poured the foundation for his wood-fired pizza oven. The oven was the next step in the bread empire, and the intention was to start selling bread from the gate outside our home on Saturday mornings.

'Aotearoa and everything it contains was also another great love. The landscape, the culture, the community, the music, the beer, and the people. He had a great respect for all things Kiwi and so greatly wanted the country to be heading in the right direction. It was important to him to support local businesses, and he frowned upon anything entering the house that had been made or grown outside of New Zealand.

'Of course there was me! And he told me this at every opportune moment. As I continue my rollercoaster ride into the unknown, I hold on tight to his pounamu pendant (left behind that morning as he didn't want the extra sixteen grams of weight to slow him down on the climb), knowing that for ten years I was lucky to have such a great man to grow, learn, laugh and love with.

'Lastly, his most recent great love. Our baby boy, Mahe Thomas. My heart is broken at what Jamie and Mahe will not get to share. Mahe carries the genes of great mana, something

I am so thankful for.'

For his eighth birthday, Mahe wanted to visit the Remarkables for the first time. He was excited to go to the same place where his father had climbed. Understandably, Jess was nervous. This would also be her first time there.

Jess, Mahe, Shelley, and I walked up the track from the carpark to Lake Alta, with its half amphitheatre of fractured rock leading up to the summits of Single Cone and Double Cone. I pointed out some of the routes we had climbed and where the ice formed the best in winter. Not surprisingly, Mahe had lots of questions.

After checking with Jess, we ventured a little higher, all of us puffing a little from the height gain. Except for Mahe—he didn't seem to get tired at all. There were rock outcrops that we passed and, not surprisingly, Mahe wanted to scramble up each and every one of them. I glanced at Jess to make sure that what Mahe was doing was okay with her, too. It should come as no great shock that the kid was a natural.

We found harder and harder boulders to climb, Mahe running between them so he could be first to try. I attempted to keep up, to provide a semblance of protective control over the uncontainable exuberance of youth. Mahe had that bulletproof recklessness that most children possess at some stage, and I wondered if he would also be one of the lucky few who manage to carry it into their adult years.

It was a warm day. We ate lunch in the shade of an overhanging rock that had a narrow crevice running through the middle of it. Afterwards, Mahe and I managed to squeeze through the tight space.

There was a flake of rock hanging precariously over the far end of the boulder. I called out to Mahe not to use it as a hand hold.

'I know,' he answered, looking back to me and grinning a familiar grin. Then, he went back to encourage and then escort his mother through the same crack.

'Watch out for that rock, Mum,' he said protectively as Jess squeezed beneath it.

TWENTY-SEVEN

A glacier is like a tree, you said
as I hacked its melting skin
carving glass steps for tourists,
air bubbles escaped folds in the ice

In kaupapa Māori
everything has a story
Kā Roimata o Hine Hukatere, they called it
Tears of the Avalanche Girl

Her lover Wawe fell to his death here,
the weight of gravity too much,
before Cook sailed south
with his empty map

Along this angry coast
choked with thick greenery,
he remarked on two curious clouds low in the valleys
strange how their paths almost mirrored the other

You pointed out ice rings like tree rings
blue within blue, the story of the glacier
cameras can never fully capture it
timetables never quite fit

At lunch the clients fidgeted with impatience,
the glacier groaning beneath
your face wrinkled into a thin smile
the depths of a crevasse

Each day the glacier dies
just a little bit from sunlight, you said
bedrock uncovering like treasure
quartz crystals nestled in the mud

Tears of light, momentary exposure
when it rained you laughed
look!
today the glacier grows

I remember how you took up the offer
of my offhand dinner invitation,
your hand on my shoulder
two weeks before you were gone

I sit in coarse sand
as the grey sea churns,
dusk's half-light stealing memories
till I've nothing more to give,
to the go-home sound of waves
hushing in retreat
and the distant lightning
that ties ocean to cloud

Then I'm next to your mother
in view of that great, fallen trunk of ice
and she says, 'No one can hurt you now.'

For Jamie, and Marty and Denali, and Scotty, and Guy, and Howie, and others.

May the many shining mountains be a reflection of the memories we have shared with our friends, and the hope we continue to feel in ourselves.

ACKNOWLEDGEMENTS

Small portions of this book have previously appeared in various magazines, including *Alpinist*, *New Zealand Geographic*, *The Climber*, *Wilderness*, and *The Surfer's Journal*.

Thanks to the team at Di Angelo Publications: Ashley Crantas, Willy Rowberry, Stephanie Yoxen, and Kim James.

Also, thanks to Jess McLachlan, Laurence Fearnley, Matt Turner, Katie Ives, Damien Gildea, David Newstead, Graham Zimmerman, John Price, Kynan Bazley, Andrew Lindblade, Mat Woods, Aat Vervoorn, Dougal and Kirstie McKinnon, Hugh Nicholson, Dawa Lama, Derek Chinn, Rodolphe Popier, Ross Cullen, Yewjin Tan, Sequoia Schmidt, Graeme Dingle, Rob Frost, Tenzin Jorden, Danny Baillie, Scott Blackford-Scheele, Ben Dare, Kester Brown, Troy Mattingley, and Chris Marsh.

Most importantly, as always, thanks and love to Shelley Hersey.

Climb hard. Stay safe.

ABOUT THE PUBLISHER

Di Angelo Publications was founded in 2008 by Sequoia Schmidt—at the age of seventeen. The modernized publishing firm's creative headquarters is in Houston, Texas, with its distribution center located in Twin Falls, Idaho. The subsidiary rights department is based in Los Angeles, and Di Angelo Publications has recently grown to include branches in England, Australia, and Sequoia's home country of New Zealand. In 2020, Di Angelo Publications made a conscious decision to move all printing and production for domestic distribution of its books to the United States. The firm is comprised of ten imprints, and the featured imprint, Karanema, was inspired by Sequoia Schmidt, as a tribute to her Kiwi roots and to support New Zealand authors.

DI ANGELO PUBLICATIONS
A Modernized Publishing Firm

9 781955 690188